They Come Back Singing

Other Books by Gary Smith, SJ

Radical Compassion:
Finding Christ in the Heart of the Poor

Street Journal:
Finding God in the Homeless

THEY COME BACK
Singing

Finding God with the Refugees

An African Journal by **GARY SMITH, SJ**

LOYOLA PRESS.

CHICAGO

LOYOLAPRESS.

3441 N. ASHLAND AVENUE
CHICAGO, ILLINOIS 60657
(800) 621-1008
WWW.LOYOLABOOKS.ORG

Unless otherwise noted, Scripture quotations are from the Jerusalem Bible © by Darton, Longman & Todd, Ltd., and Doubleday & Company, Inc., 1966, 1967, and 1968. Reprinted with permission.

Scripture quotations marked "NRSV" are from the New Revised Standard Version Bible: Catholic Edition, copyright © 1993 and 1989 by the Division of Christian Education of the National Council of the Churches of Christ in the U.S.A. Used by permission. All rights reserved.

The excerpt from "Every Day" by Denise Levertov (p. vii) is from *Breathing the Water* (New York: New Directions Publishing, 1987), 28.

"A Noise in the Night" (pp. 85–89) was originally published as "Child Soldiers and the Lord's Resistance Army" in *America* magazine, March 29, 2004. Copyright © 2004. All rights reserved. Reprinted with permission of America Press.

"A Bridge to the Eternal" (pp. 164–70) first appeared as "The Rings of the Sitka Spruce" in *Company* magazine (Summer 2006). Reprinted with permission.

The excerpt from "Proposal" by Raymond Carver (p. 165) is from *All of Us: The Collected Poems*, copyright © 1996 by Tess Gallagher, introduction copyright © 1996 by Tess Gallagher, editor's preface, commentary, and notes copyright © 1996 by William L. Stull. Used by permission of Alfred A. Knopf, a division of Random House, Inc.

Cover photograph: David Sacks/Stone/Getty Images
Author photo: John Whitney, SJ
Maps: Bill Wood
Cover design: Kathryn Seckman Kirsch
Interior design: Tracey Sainz

Library of Congress Cataloging-in-Publication Data
Smith, Gary N., 1937–
    They come back singing : finding God with the refugees : an African journal / by Gary Smith.
        p. cm.
    ISBN-13: 978-0-8294-2701-1
    ISBN-10: 0-8294-2701-5
    1. Smith, Gary N., 1937—Diaries. 2. Catholic Church—Uganda—Clergy—Diaries. 3. Church work with refugees—Uganda. I. Title.
    BX4705.S66254A3 2008
    261.8'328096761—dc22

                                                                2007035042

Printed in the United States of America
08 09 10 11 12 13 Versa 10 9 8 7 6 5 4 3 2

For refugees everywhere

Every day, every day I hear
enough to fill
a year of nights with wondering.

—Denise Levertov, "Every Day"

Contents

Author's Note   xiii
Introduction   xvii

Part 1: Rhino Camp Refugee Settlement

Journal: August 2000   3
Killer Lightning   8
New Life, New Hope   11
Letter from Rhino Camp Refugee Settlement   14
Letter from Kampala   18
And in God There Is No Darkness at All   21
Journal: June 2001   26
A Mother's Voice Crying Out in the Wilderness   35
A Paratrooper in a Diaper   39
Letter from Arua   43
Cause of Death: Life   47
Letter from Mwanza, Tanzania   50
Journal: September 2002   54
Letter from Rhino Camp Refugee Settlement   59
Everything   62

Part 2: Adjumani Refugee Settlement

Letter from Adjumani Refugee Settlement   67
Standing Naked before an Angel   70
Journal: December 2003   76
A Noise in the Night   85

Yayo   90

The Beautiful Mouth of Jacelin Ojok   94

Journal: June 2004   104

Confirmation and Kalashnikovs   115

Letter from Nimule, Sudan   123

Holding Job in My Arms   126

Kogwon Narju   132

African Gem   138

Letter from Kampala   144

God Does Not Forget His People   147

A Love Story   154

Hakim   159

A Bridge to the Eternal   164

Holy Week and a Cloud of Witnesses   171

A Long Night's Journey into Day   177

Say Yes Again and Forgive Forever   181

Journal: June 2005   189

The Tears of Rose Adoo   195

Journal: August 2006   202

God's Sweet Gift   210

Those Damn Jesuits   216

Afterword   223

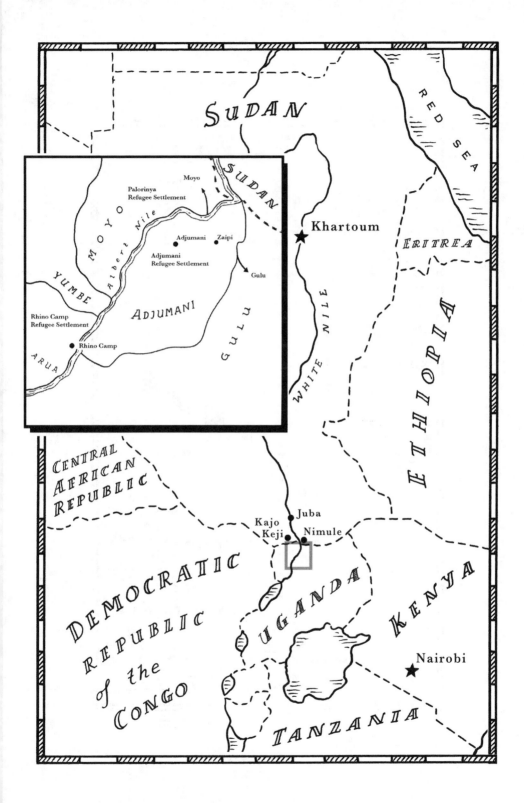

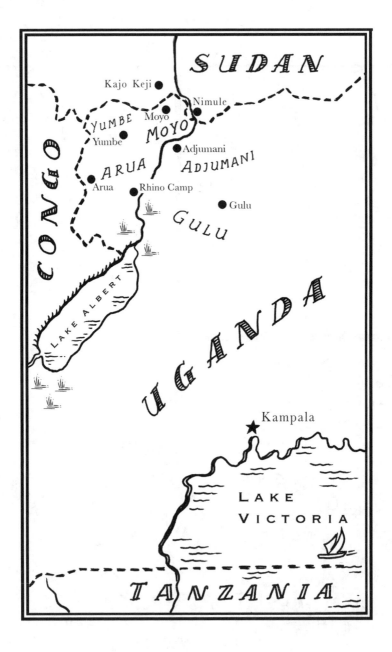

Author's Note

This is not a book about Africa. It is about my years in Africa with Sudanese refugees. It is not a sociological study of refugees; it is a portrait of refugee hearts. It is not a book about what I gave to the refugees, but a book about what they gave to me. It is not a theology of mission, but a story of mission.

I am a Catholic priest and a member of the Society of Jesus. Before entering the society, I attended college at San Jose State University and Santa Clara University. It was at San Jose State that I, an unreligious person, began—or was moved—to ask religious questions. Over a period of many months, I experienced a coalescence of extraordinary interior phenomena: a long uneven search for the meaning and purpose of my existence, a desire to end the conflict in my deepest soul between moral order and moral disorder, and an unaccountable, mysterious, and real attraction to Christ in the Gospels and in the Eucharist. This coalescence ultimately led me to Catholicism. At the University of Santa Clara, where I went to develop a theology that might help me better understand my faith, I encountered the Jesuits. I eventually chose to become a Jesuit because their following of Christ seemed to be what gave them life and love and hope in their committed service of the world. It was a big decision, one prompted by the same persistent tapping at my heart's window that had moved me toward Catholicism.

The path since then has led me through many places and experiences in this country and abroad. I was ordained a priest in the seventies.

Moved, again, to support and work with the poor, I spent the next several years in Oakland, California, as a community organizer with a team of Jesuits, helping people of poor neighborhoods organize and fight such social ills as vacant housing, drug dealing, deficient education systems, and an unresponsive city government. In the eighties, I decided to enter into the growing national issue of homelessness and went to Tacoma, Washington, to serve as the director of Nativity House, a drop-in center for street people and the homeless. In the nineties, continuing my street ministry, I worked with inmates in jails and with residents—especially the mentally ill—of low-income residential hotels in downtown Portland, Oregon. After eight years in Portland, living in the heart of the inner city, I was moved once again to think in a new direction.

Here is what happened: One night in Portland, as I was chatting with friends over pizza and beer, reflecting out loud about my ministry and life, I expressed to them—and, I guess, to myself, as I tapped into emerging realizations—that I wanted to be with the poor in a different way. Life was becoming too comfortable. I was feeling, I thought—and here it comes again—an invitation, a prompting to something more. Someone mentioned Kierkegaard, the nineteenth-century Danish existentialist theologian and philosopher, who talked about the "truth which is true for me," for which he could live and die. Kierkegaard emphasized the movement of faith in a person's heart, and the subsequent choices that take the individual into untraveled country, beyond the expectations and laws of religious structures and beyond the safe world of one's everyday life and actions. As we talked about this "true idea," I thought of a conversation I'd had months before with a Jesuit at a Baltimore meeting on domestic social justice issues. He had referred to the Jesuit Refugee Service (JRS) and its commitment to the refugees of the world. Recalling that conversation suddenly brought into focus everything that had been swimming around in me: the sense of wanting to do more, the desire to identify my "true idea," and the awareness of the world's cry for help. I mentioned the conversation to my friends. "Is serving the refugees an idea worth living and dying for?" someone asked. "And isn't it true that the Jesuits should be where no one else goes?"

After we broke up, I slipped gently into a night of thought and prayer, staring up at the ceiling, listening to the sounds of the inner city, pondering my heart's questions, tracking the way I was praying. There was something going on, a movement at the door of my heart. I knew the rhythm and insistence of that knock: God seeking entrance. It was not an agitated movement, but rather one of peace. *What about the refugees of the world? Could I serve them?* I lived in the presence of these questions for days, watching where my passion was moving, gauging whether I was at peace, and eventually talking it over with my spiritual director and one of my dearest Jesuit friends, Andy Dufner. Dufner always had a way of helping me see if I was on a quixotic pursuit or being touched cleanly and clearly by the gentle way of God. Eventually, we agreed that all the signs made sense, and I went to my provincial and laid it out in front of him. It was a tough conversation: he knew me and my ministry, and he loved me and did not want to lose me from the province. But he agreed with my discernment and recognized and named what appeared to be a "call." With his blessing, I spoke to a JRS-connected friend in Washington, DC. Phone calls followed. An application was sent. The answer came: there is a place in Africa. In Uganda.

I never regretted the decision to go to the Sudanese refugee settlements of Uganda. I knew from the outset that it was uncharted territory for me and would be risky. But my entire life had been one of moving into unknown situations: converting to Catholicism; entering the Jesuit order; teaching high school; ministering in men's and women's prisons; organizing on the streets of Oakland; living among the poor and homeless of Tacoma and Portland; learning new languages and cultures in Mexico and Bolivia, China and Spain; loving and being loved by good and bad alike. Uganda was just another unpredictable endeavor in the unfolding mystery of my life, where I encountered a new culture, was challenged to break open the Gospel in a new way, and had to face my strengths and shortcomings once again. In short, following Christ in the service of Sudanese refugees became the idea for which I was willing to live and die. From the moment I landed on that dirt runway in northern Uganda, I trusted that God was with me, calling me, desiring me, comforting me. I trusted that God would disclose what I was to be in this new world.

I started thinking about this book in the latter part of my second year in Uganda. To stay sane and focused in the stressful and demanding world of the refugee settlements, I journaled. Often it was too hot to write anything but a few notes, to be expanded upon when I could manage a break in the cooler climates of Kampala, hundreds of miles south. This book emerged from those journal writings. I wanted to take a reader into the life of the refugees, to show how I came to know and serve them and how they changed me. I wrote this book, too, because I feel that my Jesuit life includes the invitation to express what makes my heart tick. Finally, I wrote this to share my story with all who want to attend to and understand the broad and benevolent movements of the heart that I believe are born of the heart of God.

After learning that JRS would be sending me to Africa, I sat at my desk and pondered the enormity of it all. Hosea 11:1 rose in my thoughts:

> When Israel was a child I loved him,
>   and I called my son out of Egypt.

In the spirit of Hosea, the story that follows is about a child loved and called. It is a story about the people who helped me make sense of that call and who taught me the meaning of that love.

Introduction

Uganda is an East African country that straddles the equator and is about the size of the state of Oregon. It is a landlocked nation, surrounded by the Democratic Republic of the Congo on the west, Sudan on the north, Kenya on the east, and Rwanda and Tanzania on the south. With a population of twenty-eight million, Uganda, at this writing, hosts nearly one hundred thousand Sudanese refugees in its northern tiers, those areas bordering Sudan.

Sudan, in northeastern Africa, is a huge country, roughly one-fourth the size of the United States, with a population estimated at thirty-six million. It has a twisted and painful history involving several internal wars, often between the Arabs of the North and the sub-Saharan tribes of the South. Part of the conflict is religious—the Muslim North versus the Christian-animist South—and part of it is political, over who controls the oil fields of Sudan. The brutal civil war in Sudan between the government in Khartoum in the North and the Sudan People's Liberation Army (SPLA) in the South began in the 1980s. It is estimated that as many as two million died in the war, and another four million were displaced. Hundreds of thousands of escaping refugees came south into Uganda. Most had little choice. They could either remain in Sudan and face possible death or flee into the uncertain world of exile.

As a result, over the years, several refugee settlements were established in Ugandan administrative districts. Within these settlements are many villages, set up by the Office of the United Nations High Commissioner for Refugees (UNHCR). Most Sudanese refugees in Uganda live in the three northern districts—Adjumani, Moyo, and Arua—and within a hundred miles of the Sudan border. In the Adjumani district, on the east side of the Nile River, is the Adjumani Refugee Settlement, in which there are thirty villages. In the Moyo district, on the west side of the Nile, is the Palorinya Refugee Settlement, in which there are twenty-one villages. The Rhino Camp Refugee Settlement, in the Arua district, contains nineteen villages. It lies to the west of the Nile and south of the Adjumani and Palorinya settlements.

Within the refugee villages live Sudanese people of numerous tribes, most with their own distinct language. A number of nongovernmental organizations, or NGOs, work with the UNHCR to implement various refugee programs, in education or in health and medicine or in the construction of water facilities. These NGOs are called implementing partners and receive part of their program funding from their mother organizations outside of the country and part from the UNHCR. The Jesuit Refugee Service (JRS) is one such implementing partner, focusing on pastoral and educational matters.

My education in Sudanese culture often came during the events surrounding Sunday morning Mass, or "Prayers," in a particular village. (Sudan is 75 percent Muslim. Most of the refugees in Uganda are Christians.) There was always a striking sense of welcome, from the time I drove into a village and throughout Prayers and the meal that followed. The expression "You are most welcome," in the tribal language, in Arabic, or in English, was freely and frequently uttered, a reflection of the cultural value of hospitality toward visitors and travelers, known or unknown. The Sudanese cultural landscape includes a multitude of languages, and I would often hear three or four different tongues in a village, though each village in a refugee settlement is usually created along tribal and linguistic lines. Here the Bari, there the Dinka, down the road the Madi, and so forth. The singing at Mass sometimes went beyond that, incorporating even music in Lingala, a Congolese language acquired by some refugees who escaped into Congo before moving on to Uganda. The Sudanese love to sing and dance. It was always amazing to me to see the instant unified movement of bodies and hear the polyphonic singing of the entire congregation at Prayers, as if they had practiced all night. Music and dance are part of the Sudanese soul, and I was often brought to tears by the beauty and spontaneity of it all.

After Mass, there was usually a meal. The food was always simple: tea, a few small fish, perhaps some beans, and a bread called posho, made of maize and sorghum. You were to eat the posho with your right hand after washing your hands in a basin of water poured by the host. Before we ate, whether the meal was a cup of water or a plate of fish or a piece of bread, we had a prayer of thanksgiving, reflecting the deep faith that permeates the Sudanese culture. This prayer was one of gratitude in spite of heartbreaking personal and material deprivations; it was one of gratitude for the simplest of gifts, for being alive and for having escaped the war in Sudan.

The pecking order of the culture is also revealed at meals: the men and elders (women or men) are served by the young people of the chapel. The Sudanese culture is patriarchal but is gradually being transformed by a growing number of educated women, including some strong women catechists who lead their chapels in Prayers and Christian education.

The people are personable, and there was much laughter (you can hear Sudanese laughing at great distances) when we ate, especially if someone was poking fun at him- or herself. One day I joked about regularly hitting my head on the low entrances of chapels and thatched huts called tukuls, seemingly incapable of learning the simple act of ducking. You'd have thought I was the funniest guy in the world. The conversation at meals would attend to a variety of topics: the war, the village, education for the children, babies born, deaths (especially from malaria), drought or rain and planting and harvesting (most of the culture is agricultural), struggles around poverty (especially lack of food), church issues (catechist training, seminars on the faith, care for the suffering and vulnerable in the village), meetings with local Ugandan civil officials, and my own family and the American culture. The Sudanese have an oral culture; hence, much information is passed on in this way.

Early in 2005, a peace treaty was signed between the Sudanese government in Khartoum and the Sudan People's Liberation Army (SPLA) of Southern Sudan. It provided the South with autonomy for six years, after which a referendum on independence will take place. It is an uneasy peace, exacerbated by the mysterious helicopter crash, just months after the treaty was signed, that killed John Garang, the longtime leader of the SPLA and the newly appointed president of Southern Sudan. At this writing, groups of Sudanese refugees are returning to their homeland through formal repatriation sponsored by the UNHCR. Some, whose old homes were very near the border, cross over temporarily to assess opportunities and security as well as to begin constructing living quarters and preparing the ground for planting. But the majority remains in Uganda, taking a wait-and-see approach.

In addition to the hardships of life in the refugee camps, the Sudanese refugees in Uganda face another horror, that of Joseph Kony's Lord's Resistance Army (LRA). Since 1987, the LRA's armed rebellion against the Ugandan government has afflicted Ugandans in the North and, to a lesser degree, the Sudanese refugees who live there. The LRA has evolved out of the tortured history of Uganda since the country received its independence from Great Britain in 1962. From 1962 until 1986, Uganda was ruled politically and militarily by northerners, including the dictator Idi Amin, from 1971 to 1979. When the current president, Yoweri Museveni, took power through a successful rebellion, he and his comrades favored the southern and the western regions of Uganda, from where they originated.

The northern leaders fled to the bush or to Sudan, where they organized to fight Museveni. Various rebellions were mounted, only to fail and precipitate the wrath of the South and Museveni's fledgling government. One organization that emerged was a fanatical religious group claiming special inspiration from the Holy Spirit. The group called itself the Lord's Resistance Army.

The LRA's leader, Joseph Kony, proclaims himself a spirit medium whose goal is to rule Uganda under the Ten Commandments. He is opposed to Museveni and the Ugandan army, and he has attacked his own people, the Acholi, because he believes they have cooperated with the government of Uganda. The LRA has carried out its activities in the North, attacking civilians, burning and stealing property, torturing and raping village people, and abducting children. The abducted boy children are used as soldiers, and the girls are used as sex slaves. Indeed, Kony's army is essentially composed of abducted children, an estimated twenty to thirty thousand. At the height of the LRA's brutal activity, more than a million and a half northern Ugandans—Acholi people—were put into displacement camps so the government could protect them from the LRA and, as many accused, control them.

The LRA has attacked Sudanese refugee villages on the east side of the Nile, so JRS work there is compromised. The Sudanese refugees know the LRA, because for many years it had training camps in Sudan. From these camps, the LRA launched raids into northern Uganda. The governments of Sudan and Uganda have accused each other of violating their common frontier and supporting the other's insurgents. Diplomatic relations between the two countries were severed in 1995, allegedly because of Sudan's support of the LRA in retaliation for Uganda's participation in the Sudanese government's war against the SPLA. Normal relations were restored in 1999–2000. In the summer of 2006, representatives from the LRA and the Ugandan government began peace talks in Juba, Sudan, brokered by the government of Southern Sudan. Their negotiations have been contentious and continue at this writing.

The Jesuit Refugee Service has been in northern Uganda since 1993. JRS was born in November 1980 when the superior general of the Jesuits, Pedro Arrupe, distressed by the tragic conditions of refugees around the world and specifically the Vietnamese "boat people," determined that the Jesuits should be involved as an organization in relief, planning, and resolution efforts. To do so, the Jesuits would utilize their worldwide talents and resources. Decades later, JRS works in more than fifty countries, functioning in administrative regions that can include several countries. Its mandate is to accompany, serve, and advocate for refugees, for those displaced within their own countries, and for asylum seekers. It is composed of about seventy-five members of the Society of Jesus from various countries and seventy-five religious of other congregations, working with approximately one thousand indigenous people. JRS works in the areas of education, advocacy, emergency assistance, pastoral services, health and nutrition, income-generating activities, and social services. The organization strives to be a nourishing and encouraging heart at the bends in the refugee trail, to walk with refugees along their journey, to offer a hand for the next part of the climb to freedom, and to say to refugees—by word and action—that they are not forgotten.

I was a staff person in the Ugandan JRS project for six years. The Ugandan and Sudanese projects are directed from a country office in Kampala, which in turn is directed by the regional JRS office in Nairobi, Kenya. The JRS Eastern Africa office oversees projects in Uganda, Kenya, Tanzania, Sudan, Somalia, and Ethiopia. During my time in Uganda, I worked first in the Rhino Camp Refugee Settlement for two and a half years, and then in the Adjumani and Palorinya settlements for three and a half years. My job was in the pastoral area, and I was charged with accompanying, serving, and advocating for the people in the villages of these settlements.

Part I

Rhino Camp
Refugee Settlement

Journal: August 2000

Touching Down in Africa

I arrived in Kenya at 10:00 p.m., after a hopscotch flight from Portland to Seattle to Amsterdam to Nairobi. The airport was unwelcoming in the night. I expect lots of lights and hustle and bustle at airports, but there was little activity at that hour in the dim and gloomy Nairobi airport terminal.

Welcome to Africa.

I was nervous. I barely acknowledged the JRS contact person when he called my name as I left customs.

The air outside the airport was cold, biting, and drizzly, but things warmed up when I walked into the welcoming Jesuit community. Still, I felt a slight depression—or was it anxiety? Maybe I am scared. I must continually revisit my intentions in coming here: to place myself into God's hands, to offer my skills to refugees, and to deepen my desire to serve the poor. I cannot allow myself to be seduced by the army of potential catastrophes marching through my head, including death. If God brought me to Africa for that, so be it.

Lead me, O God. In all this, craft a steady heart.

Shopping in Kampala

After a brief meeting with the JRS Eastern Africa director in Nairobi, I flew to Kampala, about an hour-long trip. My assignment: to serve as the assistant to the JRS project director in the Rhino Camp Refugee Settlement, in northern Uganda. But I will have a few days in Kampala to acclimate to the scene. Given all the nutty and impossible situations that have dotted my life, I am always amazed at how unsure I am in new surroundings. It's like an outlaw gene has been unleashed inside me and sends a message of self-doubt to my heart. Here I am, starting over *again*. And doubting myself. I am about to walk onto one of the great stages of the suffering world, presuming that I can use my few talents in service of the refugees.

After Mass with the Jesuit community, I was in tears. Why? I was overwhelmed with fear, hope, gratitude. I snapped out of it when I went shopping in Kampala with Paco, the Mexican Jesuit with whom I will be working. He came down from Rhino Camp to shop for a few necessities and to accompany me back. He is a good guy and a wheel of energy. He will be leaving JRS soon, and I will probably be taking over as project director.

Impressions of Kampala: streets seething with young men, cars, taxis packed with people, prostitutes giving me the come-and-get-it nod, motorbikes and traffic police, beggars crawling on deformed legs, and mothers carrying their babies on their backs. Walking from the Jesuit residence to the center of town, I passed a traffic jam and hundreds of sidewalk merchants selling old Sunday magazine sections of the *Monitor* and the *New Vision* (the English-language Ugandan newspapers), worn-out and frayed books, peanuts, bananas, pineapple slices, handkerchiefs, watchbands, Bibles, pens, and cheap socks. Giant garbage-eating storks were flying around, pterodactyl-like, coming to rest on the top of buildings and trees, where they casually took in the scene below, like they were meditating. I walked by security people standing and sitting vigil in front of banks, money-exchange places, markets, jewelry stores—in a word, any place that has money. They cradled automatic rifles and sawed-off shotguns and exhibited cold and unimpressed faces. Huge waves of noise and people and activity constantly broke over me as I cautiously made my gawking way down the street.

I was nearly clobbered by two cars. In Uganda, cars drive on the left side, and rarely do you have the luxury of pedestrian crosswalks. Or stoplights. I looked the wrong way, stepped out into the street, bounced backward to avoid a honking truck, and then was almost run down by a taxi coming fast from the other direction.

I struggle emotionally off and on, and I spend too much of my time concerned about the future and living in the glory of the past. I wind up praying in the night, asking God to assist me in seizing these new moments in my life and to help me see that here, in this new land, God will give me new gifts; here I will learn deeper trust and new ways to use my talents.

Arriving at Rhino Camp

Paco and I flew from Kampala to Arua in a two-engine, twelve-seat grasshopper of a plane. The distance is 350 miles, almost directly north, and the flight takes ninety minutes. We made a brief stop in Pakuba, a town on the shores of Lake Albert, which Uganda shares with the Democratic Republic of the Congo. We buzzed the runway once to chase off the giraffes that use it as a shortcut.

The landing in Arua, the largest northwestern Ugandan town, fifteen miles from the eastern border of Congo, was smooth, but I was antsy as we made the approach to the dirt runway. We were greeted there by the JRS staff of Rhino Camp Refugee Settlement and a few refugee leaders. From Arua, we drove for an hour and a half to the settlement and the JRS compound. I rested, ate, and was introduced to my new home. The fifty-by-fifty-yard compound consists of four thatch-covered houses called tukuls, a latrine, a place for bathing, a small building for storage called "the store," an open charcoal-fueled kitchen, a small eating facility, a well for water (called a borehole), an anemic thatched carport for the pickup, lots of willowy neem trees, and three ducks. We had a good evening meal and I retired early, obsessively checking to make sure the mosquito net was hanging properly.

In the morning, Paco and I toured the Rhino Camp Refugee Settlement, roughly two hundred square miles in size. The settlement is so named because it is adjacent to the Ugandan town of Rhino Camp, which sits on the west bank of the Nile River. The rhinos were hunted to extinction in the last century, so the name is misleading. The town of Rhino Camp is small, located fifty miles east of Arua. A few thousand Ugandans live there, subsisting off the land. Rhino Camp is also home to a small fish industry; each day fish from the Nile are trucked or biked to the Arua market.

In the early nineties, the UNHCR, in concert with the Ugandan government, established the Rhino Camp Refugee Settlement for Sudanese fleeing their civil war. Eventually, forty-one villages were established in the settlement, and the thirty-five thousand refugees who live there are placed among the villages primarily by tribal and language lines. Most of the refugees are Christian, and constructing a small chapel was one of the first things each village did. In a few villages, the people pray under a huge tree rather than in a chapel, either because they could not afford to build one or because their wood-and-thatch chapel collapsed from termite attacks. All the people of the villages in the refugee settlement are subject to the Ugandan government and are directed by a government-appointed settlement commander. His is the last word on virtually everything, from crime to new construction to traveling permits out of the settlement.

Paco and I moved quickly through each village, where we were briefly received, sometimes by only the chapel elders, sometimes by the elders and enthusiastic crowds of curious people, sometimes by all the above plus a small army of smiling children, singing and dancing songs of welcome. The villages are tattoos on my heart: Agulupi, Aligoi, Ariwa, Eden, Kaligo, Katiku, Kiriadaku, Mariaba, Matangacia, Ngurua, Ocea, Odobu, Olujobo, Ossa, Simbili, Siripi, Tika, Walope, Wanyange, and Yelulu—each a memory of faces and events.

Despite the big welcomes and the warmth of my colleagues here, I have been nervous ever since I left Portland. Everything is new, and I am working hard to absorb all the places and faces and greetings. I am conscious of the language differences, and I wonder if I'll ever be able to lead people in Prayers in their own language. Once again, I am second-guessing myself: Am I strong enough to deal with a new culture and its physical challenges? Will I be able to help out with the programs Paco has efficiently established, especially those, like catechist training, income-generating activities, and adult education, about which I know very little? I am Mr. Street Guy from the USA—my expertise is in other areas. And will I be able to communicate with the people? Even my English, laced as it is with a million street idioms, is often unintelligible even to Paco, who is Mexican but totally fluent in English.

Back at the JRS compound, I went to my internal mountaintop to pray to God to help me overcome my temptations to self-doubt. But it is not all darkness and gloom. I am consoled to be surrounded by the refugees, who are clearly happy that I am here. My God, I am here. I am in Uganda. I am among the refugees.

Killer Lightning

It was a November storm and my first in Rhino. At one point, a bolt of lightning and a clap of thunder arrived at once, an explosion that left me hunched over, heart pounding. The lightning had been close. It struck about fifty yards away from my tukul.

And it killed a human being.

The man was walking just west of the JRS compound, on a worn trail that snaked through the countryside and linked up with a road in front of our property. He was pushing his bike as he walked. Ten yards ahead of him, pushing her own bike, was his wife, a baby strapped to her back and three other children following her.

Shortly after the blast, a Sudanese man who was in the area ran to the compound and notified the three of us who were home—Paco, George Atibuni, and me—that a man had been struck by lightning. Could we come right away?

We arrived at the place where the rigid figure lay on the muddy ground. His black skin was burned off from shoulders to waist, giving the appearance of a half albino. Dead. His wife stood a few yards away, staring at the body of the man who, until twenty minutes before, had been her mate of many years. She was stunned, shivering in the rain, her baby crying—an eerie sound in the numb silence of those who had come to the scene. Nothing could have snapped the woman out of her trance. Incredibly, a chicken, tied at the legs, which had been brought for food later in the day, was hanging upside down on the handlebars of the man's bike, alive and twitching, with half of its feathers burned off. How strange: the man dead, his body blasted into rigor mortis by a lightning bolt, and the chicken, inches away from the man at the moment of impact, still alive, thrashing around on the front of the bike.

Surrounded by the Ugandan nationals who live near the JRS compound, Paco and I had a brief conversation and then sent Atibuni, a Ugandan himself, to notify the appropriate official. The speed and tragedy of this death invaded me. It turned out that this couple was Sudanese and had seven children. They and their four youngest children were headed to Yelulu, a nearby village in the settlement, to work in the fields with the couple's adult children, who had families of their own.

A Ugandan policeman came, one who works with the local refugees, and said, after a short examination, that it was all right to take the body and bury it. There would be no official postmortem, as there are no coroners in this part of the world. Even if the man had survived, there are no doctors or hospitals around here where he could have been taken. So, in the heavy rain, the people placed the body, enshrouded in a blanket I had taken from my room, into the bed of our pickup with three of the children. The wife and the baby, along with Atibuni and a man who had been traveling with the family, rode in the cabin—along with the chicken. The woman had asked for the chicken as we were loading up because it could still be eaten. The fact of hunger is always present, even in consuming sadness. They set off on a two-hour drive to the couple's home village on slippery, rain-soaked roads.

Like most deaths in this part of the universe, this man's was sudden, leaving much up in the air in terms of what the family will do in the long term. But the community will gather and will care for and comfort the widow and her children in the immediate future.

This mess captures what it means to be a refugee in this part of the world that is invisible to developed nations. These two poor people, a father and a mother, a husband and a wife, traveled by bike on a rainy day to fields miles and miles from their home, bearing their youngest child, with three more children on foot, and a chicken to be killed and cooked for the day's only meal. They traveled through the bush, with no paved roads and no toilets or water along the way, in the hot sun, subject to sudden storms, dodging opportunistic mosquitoes. And then he was killed, dead in his tracks. There were no phones around to call the next of kin, no government officials to sign a cause-of-death certificate, and no emergency vehicles to pick up the body. He was simply wrapped in a blanket and taken home, to be buried next to his small family tukul, his wife and children and friends mourning for three days.

Death in the Rhino Camp Settlement: it is everywhere. People do not live long enough to die gracefully in their old age. Children die all the time. Talk to any refugee parent, and he or she will tell you. Lucy Kaigi has had twelve kids; six of them have died. Steven Asega lost his first three children. Theopista, on our staff, is one of thirteen children; only she and her brother survived. Every family has lost at least one. Cause of death? Disease mainly, those diseases that invade malnourished bodies. All live intimately with death, like this widow, her husband struck dead ten yards behind her. I saw her about two weeks later, and she was frighteningly stoic about it all. Stunned, yes, and bewildered, but there was resignation on her prematurely aged face; even the death of her man was just one more grinding instance of suffering that has accompanied her life, like stunted trees along the road.

Africa can be an alternate world sometimes. This is not the safe and protected world I left. I am constantly reminded of this.

So, my God, death again. I pray for this man, for his family. Bless him as he now comes to you, as we all will come to you, naked and bewildered. Comfort his family and send helpful people into their lives. Show me how to be present in this death, and what I am to learn.

New Life, New Hope

On Christmas Eve, as darkness came, I celebrated Mass in the village of Agulupi. It was a hot night, and there were maybe seventy people in the little thatch-covered chapel. Dust covered everything, and I could smell the sweat of the people who were crowded cheerfully into the room. A kerosene lamp hung on a wooden pillar to the right of the altar. Huge moths periodically crashed into the lamp, and once in a while one could hear the slap of a hand as another mosquito made a hungry landing.

Students sang the liturgy's rich music, and twenty grade-school girls danced around the altar. Agulupi is home to many Sudanese who fled to Uganda via Congo, and after communion the singers began a Christmas song in Lingala, the language of eastern Congo, that featured an imitation of the wailing of the baby Jesus. The dancers sighed while folding their forearms over their foreheads in an expression of weeping. It cut straight to my heart: a cry heard down through the centuries from God-become-human; and, too, an echo of the wailing of refugees who have endured a long road of flight and suffering. As with that birth in a barn, there is a sense in all this stinking poverty of hope reborn.

I said the Mass in Bari, which most present could understand, and gave the homily in English, which was translated into Arabic, which all could understand. After Mass, the people, flashing smiles and tired eyes, presented me with my Christmas gift: a live duck. Food for life. Is there a better gift? Earlier in the day, seven miles away by a dirt road, in a village called Wanyange, after another Eucharist, the people gave me seven eggs.

The night was full of contrasts for me: the absence of loved ones and the presence of welcoming refugees; the deprivation of the settlement and the wealth of faith; the longing for home and the comfort of the Eucharist. I thought often of Christ's words: "This is my body, given to you; this is my blood, poured out for you." Those words have always contained for me the tenderness found also in the moment of his birth: here was a child, born as a mission of care and love from the heart of God. On that Christmas Eve in obscure Agulupi, Jesus was born again, his tender presence hidden in the bread, nourishing me and the little congregation.

Even as I clung to the familiarity of the Eucharist, I celebrated this Mass as if it were my first. And it was, in a sense: everything feels new in these new surroundings and this new culture. It is startling, the new-ness of it all. It takes time to adjust to a night like this, but there is no time, because I have been thrust into an utterly foreign world, and I have to respond. There are so many moments like this here: adjustments to food, lack of clean water, creatures of the night, customs, relationships, expectations, suffering children, unrelenting heat, absence of loved ones, unforgiving terrain, unexpected disease, death, and requests for help that are heartbreaking in their simplicity and impossibility. And yet I take refuge in the consolation of Christ once again pouring out his love and hope in the Christmas mystery as I face what is new and frightening and unclear.

The promise of Christmas was brought home for me powerfully on Christmas Day. I spent it with two young men, Kingara and Otumbara, students I had met shortly after arriving at Rhino and who were home from school for the holiday. After Christmas Eve Mass, they had approached me, in a crowd of secondary school kids home for the break, all of whom speak English and were eager to talk, and invited me to join them for Christmas tea. Kingara and Otumbara are good kids, honest and guileless, orphaned by the civil war. We sat on the dirt floor of their tukul sipping tea and eating chocolate chip cookies I had received from a friend in the States (they were hard as rocks but dunkable). Many other teenagers had crowded into the tukul. They all knew and admired Kingara and Otumbara, both bright and determined to find a way to continue their education. They never knew their fathers and barely knew their mothers, escaping from Sudan as young teenagers, their families slaughtered. We talked at length; they asked lots of questions about my country, my family, and education in the States. They had a difficult time grasping that my mother tongue was English, since they understood it to be an international language to be learned, as they had learned it, after the acquisition of one's native language. I was curious about their escape from Sudan and their hopes for the future. After the other teenagers left, I gave Kingara and Otumbara each a calculator, decent ones I had purchased in Arua. They were flabbergasted and grateful. As I left, we planned to meet again during their next school break, in April.

Like Mary and Joseph, Kingara and Otumbara are simultaneously being born and giving birth in a foreign land. In their quest for an education, and for truth, they are claiming their lives and their hearts, bringing new life and new hope to their continent and to their Sudanese culture. It is a similar situation for me. Far from home and from my loved ones, I am being born anew, through the grace of the One who created and sustains me.

Letter from Rhino Camp Refugee Settlement

Dear P.,

Hi, dear friend. Where to begin? It has been a slow and fast, serious and hilarious adjustment. The trip from Portland to East Africa, which you have experienced, was uneventful. The free wine on the flight helped take the edge off the emotional pain of farewells and the weariness of being stuffed into an airplane seat for sixteen hours. Our brothers, the African Jesuits in Nairobi and Kampala, were warm in their reception, though no amount of welcome can ease the anxiety of entering a completely foreign culture. I was like Paul finally arriving in Macedonia, saying to myself, *Well, I am here because you have called me here. Now what?* There have been some tough moments, partly a result of the cultural adaptation. But there is also the constant struggle to trust in God in my anxiety, and the drain of having to be an extrovert when I am by nature an introvert, and the absence of friends and spoken love.

After delays in Kampala because of an Ebola scare in northern Uganda and rebel ambushes to the east of my assigned location, I flew north to Arua, a town fifteen miles east of Congo and perhaps fifty miles south of Sudan. I came up with a Mexican Jesuit, Paco, who is the director of the JRS project in Rhino Camp Settlement. He is a veteran: five years in Africa and decades in the jungles of Chiapas and the slums of Mexico City. He is a talented man, wiry of body and mind, used to working alone. He tends to have a short fuse, although he learned quickly that anger doesn't work on me, so he has had to adjust. In the end, I don't think my strength will threaten him; indeed, it can be the basis of a companionship that he has not had for some time. He will be leaving the project soon, I am told.

Meeting us at the Arua airstrip were the three other JRS staffers, Atibuni, Lodu, and Lokuri, all young laymen, one Ugandan and two Sudanese. They are excellent people who have been helpful in my adjustment and education. From Arua, we bumped our way along a fifty-mile dirt road to the Rhino Camp Refugee Settlement, my home for the next few years.

The land is bush country, with lots of grass and low-rising trees. I arrived at the outset of the dry season, and the heat is like a lamprey that sucks the life out of you. In the dry season, not much in the way of subsistence crops can grow. Malaria is prevalent here; knowing this is like living in a house with a smoldering fire in the basement; one is always waiting for the flames to make their move. Everyone here has had and will have malaria. It is the very young who suffer the most from it. Almost one million children under the age of five in sub-Saharan Africa die each year from the disease.

I have all the conveniences of home: no electricity, no plumbing, no phone, no running water, and no TV (but I do have my handy-dandy shortwave radio). I have a blessedly long bed with a mosquito net. I live in a little one-room thatch-covered house called a tukul, which I share with lizards, fleas, dive-bomber moths, grasshoppers, spiders, mosquitoes, plump cockroaches, and a million what-the-hell-is-that creepy crawlers. Your kind of place. There are snakes, too, including cobras and black mambas. Even a "shower" is an adventure and an act of will, since one has to maneuver with buckets, cups, and a twenty-liter "Jeri can" (named after the British nickname for the Germans, who produced it during World War II). The food is very difficult for me, and already my mind wanders off into frequent food fantasies. What I would give for a green salad and a piece of cheddar cheese.

The JRS work in the Rhino Camp Settlement is primarily pastoral, while other projects in northern Uganda and Southern Sudan emphasize education. There is an educational component here as well, although it is directed toward adult literacy. The Rhino Camp project also is committed to the development of cooperatives, as refugees endeavor to establish small businesses to compensate for the consistently infertile land. A big investment on the part of JRS is in the training of Catholic leadership: elders, catechists, youth, and women. And we celebrate the Eucharist and other sacramental activities in nineteen different chapels. I have baptized more children in two months than I have in my entire thirty years as a priest. I go to the villages for Mass either on a motorcycle (Gary Smith, born to be wild!) or in a pickup. The catechists who work with me in the chapels usually translate my English homily into Arabic or Bari, a Sudanese language. I am beginning to learn the Mass in Bari. Some days, there may be four different languages we have to work with. The liturgies are full of nonstop dancing and singing and rich in faith and a sense of trust in God. It always touches me.

Incidentally, I have seen more exposed breasts in my few weeks here than I have in my entire life. Mothers breast-feed during baptisms, and in anointing so many little nursing heads I sometimes wind up anointing heads and breasts in one, uh, *graceful* movement. Life and cultures are so relative. I realized one day that I was baptizing three babies of separate mothers but all having the same daddy. It doesn't happen often, but it happens. Polygamy is a cultural nut that the African church has not yet figured out how to crack.

The people are good and welcoming; they possess a deep faith and are resilient in the face of crushing obstacles. Never have I heard the

Twenty-third Psalm—The Lord Is My Shepherd—prayed with such devotion in the midst of absolutely oppressive surroundings. But faith never softens the reality of deprivation. The deepest lash to my soul is the suffering of the children. Disease makes its move early; the life expectancy here is just over forty. There are all kinds of hideous things: malaria, worms, TB, typhoid, dysentery, cholera, tropical ulcers, and leprosy. Not to mention the payback to the body for years of backbreaking work, never having a permanent home, and grief over family separations. Like street people in the States used to tell me, "It's not the years that age you, Father; it's the miles." The Sudanese have traveled lots of miles.

To preach to this sea of suffering is like learning how to talk again. Herein lies a sobering truth: I am free when I am out of control, when I get out of the way and let those walls come down. I cannot depend on clever idioms and flashy rhetoric when breaking open the Gospel. Often, if I slip into Americanisms, the translators have no idea what I'm talking about, even if they *have* figured out the difficult American accent. The stripping that occurs is not of conveniences; it is of old ways of operating. So humility comes thundering into my life in spite of myself. Or maybe God is in the hunt for my humility. I was deeply immersed in that truth on Christmas Eve at the small village of Agulupi. In their chapel lit by a kerosene lamp, there was a moment when I looked at the bread and said to myself, *This is me: offered, broken, and shared.* The truth is that I am dependent on a power bigger than any talents I bring to the situation. In fact, my talents here sometimes don't mean shit. I was, P., at that moment, looking at my life, and I knew, like Jeremiah, that I was seized by "a fire burning in my heart, / imprisoned in my bones" (20:9).

I did not start the fire, and I am not sure I can control how much heart fuel will be burned.

Greet the community. I send my prayers and love to all of you.

Gary

Letter from Kampala

Dear R.,

Hi. It was good to hear from you. I write this from Kampala, where I'm taking a break from the North. It gives me a chance to clear my head, have a few hot showers, eat better food, and do the shopping. The flight from Arua, which has the closest airstrip to the Rhino Camp Refugee Settlement, to Entebbe Airport, about thirty miles outside of Kampala, takes about an hour and a half. The approach over Lake Victoria is breathtaking. I get down about every three months and stay with the ten Jesuits at the community in Kampala. I miss all of you and read your letters over and over again.

You asked about the wars that affect us in northern Uganda. I'll try to give you an overview. The JRS projects in the north of Uganda and in Southern Sudan labor under the dark shadow of war. Rhino is not directly involved, but of course all the refugees here have family still in Sudan. The civil war there staggers along. It has bled that poor country for almost twenty years. The Sudanese government, in white-hot anger over recent rebel successes, has taken to bombing villages along the border—in Rhino, we can hear the Russian-built Antonov bombers make their sweeping turns over Ugandan territory. Whenever the planes fly overhead, the refugees get a certain look on their faces. They have been there. They know.

In Uganda, there is also the festering rebellion of a malignantly charismatic nutcase by the name of Joseph Kony, who is the self-proclaimed leader of the Lord's Resistance Army (LRA). He says he receives visions and instructions from God. The LRA specializes in destruction and mayhem, ambushing a bus here and a truck there, burning down schools and hospitals, invading and torching displacement camps, killing indiscriminately, and, worst of all, abducting many children, who are forced to become soldiers and sex slaves. As far as I can figure, there is no coherent ideological component in their fight, but rather a combination of Christian fundamentalism and opposition to Museveni's government. LRA rips and runs on the other side of the Nile from Rhino, so we are not affected directly, though we are touched by fleeing Ugandans who escape over to the west side of the Nile. The stories about LRA activities are horrific. Most recently, they stopped a bus, pulled the people out, put padlocks through their lips, and then torched the bus.

But there is another side of my life here, a counterpoint to the depressive and destructive activities of the LRA: it is the richness of the people and the joy that being among them brings. Recently, at a Sunday Mass, during the prayers of the people, a woman was uttering a fervent prayer for rain. A six-year-old boy stepped into the middle of the aisle, maybe ten feet away from the altar, and proceeded to take the pee of the century on the parched dirt floor, looking at me with a stare somewhere between defiance and ecstasy. Of course, the whole chapel started cracking up, including the woman who was praying for rain. She was the mother of this kid. Sort of gives new meaning to the efficacy of prayer, doesn't it?

Another time, two seven-year-old Acholi girls were discussing me as they stood behind my chair outside the chapel at the village of Ariwa. I was talking to several of the village elders at the time. One of them, who spoke excellent English, asked me if I would like to know what the children were saying. I nodded, and he gave the following running translation, the girls unaware that I was eavesdropping on their animated conversation, which was interspersed with lots of giggling:

First Girl: He is very tall.

Second Girl: Uh-huh. Imagine having to go through life like that. Have you noticed the blue eyes?

First Girl: Yes, what a handicap. How can he see? And his white skin. Scary.

Second Girl: Yes. It's like his skin is turned inside out. Very ugly. And his hair kind of makes him look like a rooster.

First Girl: Yep. Poor man.

Ugly? Rooster? Me? Hey, don't they know I'm a hunky guy?

And then one group of villagers gave me a live duck. Did I tell you that? A symbol of life and no small sacrifice. The little duck must have figured out that I am a vegetarian, because she follows me around like I am *the man*, her conquering hero.

I know you are not going to want to hear this, but I have become an insect killer. It used to be that I would kill only after intolerable levels of harassment, but the terrorism became so exasperating that I simply started going after them, figuring a good offense is a potent defense. I have killed thousands of termites, removing their little veins of mud snaking up the walls to the grass covering of my tukul, and as many ants, before they bite me and raid our food supplies. I have made tons of solo hits on spiders, wasps, flies, grasshoppers, fleas, twig bugs, scorpions, mantises, cockroaches, beetles, moths, gnats, flying white ants, dragonflies, caterpillars, mosquitoes, and all sorts of unidentifiable creepy crawlies.

I draw the line on fireflies. Too amazing to kill.

I send my love to you and the family. Remember me to all.

Much love,

Gary

And in God There Is No Darkness at All

On the night of the Easter Vigil, I walked over to Ocea, a small village about a mile from the JRS compound. It is an achingly poor community with a large number of young students, from fourteen to twenty-five years old, in grades eight to twelve. Most of them live alone and are given a slight monthly ration by the United Nations upon which to survive. Many are orphans, rendered so by a war that has killed parents and uncles and aunts, or have been separated from their families, possibly never to see them again. There are others, not orphans, who have come to Uganda seeking the more stable conditions of the education system here.

It was raining off and on, and so to create the Easter fire, three women, prominent elders in the village, stacked wood that the children had gathered at the base of a tree. How they ignited that fire in the light rain with wet wood remains a mystery to me. "African technology," a student responded to my perplexed look. From that tenderly created fire, we lit the Easter candle and moved slowly to the front of the chapel, the flame protected from the drizzle by our hands and by the thatched roof of the chapel, patched with a raggedy canvas. A group of girls danced rhythmically, leading the procession, and all present clapped and sang with a purity of faith so characteristic of these refugees. There was one kerosene lamp hanging from a eucalyptus beam over the small wooden altar, which was covered with a brilliant red and white and orange cloth.

I celebrated the Mass in Bari with snatches of Arabic. I am not fluent in either language, but one learns the language of the Mass by constant practice with patient teachers. After the Gospel was read, I had a few of the people act out the scene at the empty tomb as told in Luke 24: one woman played Mary of Magdala, another played Joanna, and another played Mary the mother of James; a few men played the roles of Peter and the apostles; and a man and a woman played the two angels who say, "Why look among the dead for someone who is alive? He is not here; he has risen." The Sudanese love drama and love to see their own people act out a drama. They can perform on the spot, much as they sing and dance.

The women were appropriately sad, fearful, and dumbfounded by the disbelieving apostles. There was a lot of laughter at this, since it pointed to the dynamic between men and women in the village. The angels, of course, brought lots of smiles, because it is amusing to see someone you know on such an intimate human level play something so celestial. The men, led by the one playing Peter, acted out the role of the confused and condescending apostles perfectly.

When the drama was over, everyone in the chapel applauded with approval, and a little tide of murmured editorial comments swept through the congregation. I asked one woman, one man, and one angel from the play to remain at the front of the chapel with me, and I asked each questions, which were translated into Arabic, about their character:

> Can you describe the tomb? How did you feel when Jesus was not there? Why were you afraid?

> Why did you and your apostle brothers not believe the women? What was going through your mind when you learned the body was gone?

Who are you, angels? Did you know where Jesus was?

And then I asked the congregation:

Where was Jesus?

Why did Jesus go through all this?

Why are we happy on this night?

What does his resurrection mean to us?

What is the relationship between our celebration here and the one in Japan, or in Rome, or in my hometown in the States?

The drama participants answered their questions with smiles and enthusiasm. When the people in the congregation answered their questions, they always stood up.

And so the Easter Vigil Scripture was broken open by old and young, and the ancient message of God's love was rediscovered and renewed and embraced. It was a naked and breathtaking experience for me. Here we were, in this simple little chapel, with its dirt floor and mud walls, a congregation of not just poor but ragged and hungry poor, and hearts were being expressed, passionately and innocently. I thought of the line uttered by the British bureaucrat protagonist in Graham Greene's *The Heart of the Matter*:

Why . . . do I love this place so much? Is it because here human nature hasn't had time to disguise itself?

The blessed poor of the Beatitudes were before me, expressing their faith with a strength emerging straight from their good hearts.

After our Eucharistic prayer, the little band of worshipers announced to me that they would escort me back to the JRS compound. So, singing and dancing—fifty strong—we plunged into the jaws of the night, a night so black that you could not see your hand in front of you were it not for the flicker of the Easter candle leading the way and a winking lantern bringing up the rear. There are no streetlamps in this part of the world.

The people sang in Arabic, Bari, a couple of Congolese dialects, English, and other languages I did not recognize. Africans negotiate languages as effortlessly as my Ocea friends moved on that dark path. I was placed in the middle of the pack, and all laughed hilariously at my every missed step to a beat and a rhythm that comes easy to the Sudanese. Incorporated into the singing at different times was "Father Gary." I don't know what they were singing, but it was done with lots of laughter, the kind that is born of love and happiness.

Imagine peering down from your magic carpet into the unyielding blackness, and there, sandwiched between a couple of small flames, you see a pack of merrymakers snaking their way along an unseen road, apparently headed for no destination other than deeper into the surrounding bush darkness.

Of course, the prevailing imagery of the Easter Vigil—Christ, the light in the darkness and the light of the world—was not lost on any of us; it was a fundamental truth that poured over us like a tropical rain. The words of the first letter of John rose in me: *God is light; there is no darkness in him at all* (1:5).

The Oceans accompanied me to the door of my tukul. What irony: the JRS mandate is to accompany these good people in the darkness of their tragic dislocation. And yet here they were, walking *me* home in the darkness.

I stood there, the crowd beaming back at me as I thanked them in Arabic and Bari and English. Then they sang again; I felt like I was being serenaded. After much singing, clapping, foot stomping, and laughter, they wished me a good night and one final "Happy Easter" and then turned and sailed back into the night. After they left, I retrieved a bottle of cheap wine from my clothes cabinet that I had stashed away for the occasion: my Easter feast. I sipped and began to let the night soak in. I could hear them off in the distance: Ocea's finest, heading home. Singing. Clapping. Banishing the night with their love of God. They were happy that I had come, but happier that on this night they could celebrate the Resurrection with the Eucharist.

> At that time Jesus exclaimed, "I bless you, Father, Lord of heaven and of earth, for hiding these things from the learned and the clever and revealing them to mere children. Yes, Father, for that is what it pleased you to do." (Matthew 11:25–26)

The night was a festival of precious images; they reside in my heart like inner icons, before which my soul can kneel and give thanks to God. I learned a lot about myself that night with my friends in Ocea: that I can be happy and relaxed in the most challenging of circumstances; that the spirit of faith exists independent of language and liturgy and church; that I am understanding what it means for a pastor to love his people and even be willing to die for them; that the simpler my life becomes, the more abundantly God comes into it. I understood deeply Paul's words to the Corinthians: "Having nothing, and yet possessing everything" (2 Corinthians 6:10, NRSV).

Journal: June 2001

Breaking the Ego

I continue to stagger through the Mass in the Bari language, and today was no exception. But the people of the village of Matangacia were grateful for the effort and that I was there. My words in English can get lost in translation, and I am constantly editing in my head before I say anything, to rid my speech of American idioms and metaphors. Breaking open the Gospel is the challenge. I will learn how to reach the heart of the people I serve; it will just take time. This place has a way of breaking the ego. I keep reminding myself that I'm not here for me or to deliver brilliant homilies. I'm here for God—period. And God will make up the difference.

The children at Mass are a joy. They normally sit in the front of the chapel on papyrus mats and are usually subdued and attentive. Sometimes an older woman will patrol the area where they sit with a long switch, just in case the kids forget where they are. When they assault me with their ear-to-ear smiles, I return the favor. At one point, with the Mass concluded, I was listening to announcements by the chapel catechist when a little girl snuck up behind me and ran her fingers through my hair. Exploring the unknown. Most of the children here have never seen a white man up close.

Ink on a Thumb

I officiated at a wedding today in the village of Siripi for which all the documentation had been done by another priest. It was full of surprises.

For starters, the couple, Paulino and Rachael, was older, not young and just starting out. Then, just before the exchange of vows, Rachael began nursing her child, who, I found out after the ceremony, was her *eighth*. After the vows, Paulino and Rachael returned to their chairs, their eyes cast down, and she resumed feeding the child. Another surprise occurred at the signing of the marriage certificate. The chapel catechist, Otim, who had done all of the translating, started painting Rachael's finger with his BIC pen. It turns out Rachael can't read or write, so her thumbprint took the place of a signature. I have certainly never seen that at weddings in the States.

The post-Mass celebration was wonderful, with waves of dancing and singing and ululating. (Ululation is a high-pitched, repetitive cry of joy or grief. The word is an onomatopoeia; the cry sounds like "Uh, lu, lu, lu.") People didn't just walk up the aisle to congratulate the couple—they *danced* up the aisle. There was a feast of beans and goat and rice and a bread called posho and tea, served by smiling women. Paulino and Rachael, a naturally shy couple, courageously endured it all, knowing that this celebration was as much for the community as it was for them—it was a communal expression of their people's love for them. As I was leaving, the married couple thanked me graciously, repeating the Bari word for "thank you," *tinate*, and then instructed each of their children to do the same, with the exception of little Mr. Hungry, who was still nursing. Finally, the new bride and groom asked for my blessing for their family. It was a wonderful day.

God's Presence in Death

Olujobo is a small village in the far eastern part of the settlement, about an hour's drive in the dry season from the JRS compound. After Eucharist this morning, the congregation and I went to the burial site of a six-year-old girl, Luwena, who had been crippled by polio from a very young age and died the previous night of malaria. Her mother, Molly, a teacher at the local primary school, was widowed by the Sudan war, and Luwena was her only child.

Almost the entire village was present. I was intimidated, walking into a crowd like that, not speaking the language and still not completely familiar with the burial customs. It was a hot, dusty, windy day, and to protect the family and me from the sun, a canvas tarp had been loosely strung over our heads. The hanging sides of the tarp, caught by the wind, flapped against the flimsy support poles. Around me stood thin Sudanese wearing faded and well-worn dresses and pants and shirts, and thongs on their feet. I was seated in front of the body, which was wrapped in a blanket and lying in front of the grave. People here are buried on the compound of their living relatives, generally next to a tukul; as I sat there, I could see many such graves: slight mounds in the ground, sometimes with a cross marker stuck into them.

I realized that day, in the midst of my feelings of intimidation and inadequacy, that my grasp of the language and my ability to deliver a few significant words were not what mattered. My presence as priest anointed the occasion. The Sudanese believe God is in all things, especially death. Being there, I, the priest, affirm their belief. It is humbling to have this conviction imposed on me. This world is so direct and raw. Like the wind in my face, I have to encounter it, engage with it, and let it sift me.

We prayed, and the child's remains were lowered into the grave, and more prayers were said. I embraced Molly. She sobbed long and hard in my arms.

The Music of Touch

The rains this week have caved in one entire side of the Ariwa chapel. This evening, we had Mass under a tree without rain. There were twenty-five first communicants; about half were young children, and the rest were adults. At the sung acclamation, after the consecration, I was overwhelmed by the beautiful polyphonic singing—it was like hearing a favorite passage in a favorite symphony. The consolation it brought me reemerged periodically throughout the morning.

At the end of Mass, I noticed a little girl, Marie by name, on the fringes of the congregation, sitting in a metal box that looked like a squat trunk. At first I thought she had just crawled in it to play. Then I realized that she was severely handicapped. Her eyes were unfocused, and her legs were merely useless appendages. "Polio caused this," her faithful sister told me, watching over Marie like a sentinel. I went over to her with Kabir, my puppet whose Arabic name means "big," and she reached out to stroke his hair. She uttered an unintelligible word in her little voice—I was informed that she does not understand language. I flashed on another severely handicapped child I knew, in a parish in San Jose, California, whose parents brought him to Mass. His father played classical music in his room all day, noting that "one never knows what is getting through." I held Marie's hand with one hand and with the other chased away the flies that were crawling over her face. Was my touch reaching her, with its own kind of music of care and love? *Ah, my little Marie, what gets through to you?*

Shopping in Arua

The staff and I traveled to Arua today for our weekly shopping and to visit the bank, which is always distressing. It is normally jammed with people, who don't stand in line but push forward en masse, and the tellers are too few and bored. After the banking, I sent a few staff to buy big-ticket items like fuel and construction materials, and I took Atibuni to the market with me. It is always good to have a native with you to negotiate prices for tomatoes or rice or oranges or eggs. It is automatic that the *muzungu*, the white man, will be charged more, so that is why I take Atibuni; he speaks Lugbara, the language of Arua, and can wheel and deal with the best of them.

One thing I can always count on in Arua is the beggars. They are generally mentally ill, handicapped, or just poor. The streets are full of them. There are three or four lepers, now cured, who always come to me. All have lost most of their fingers to the disease, so they extend only stumpy hands in supplication. Begging for alms is the only way for the handicapped to survive; the Ugandan government does not provide for them. I try to give something without making a big deal of it. All are grateful no matter what the amount.

While I was waiting in the street, leaning up against the pickup, a young boy, terribly crippled, crawled toward me, his elbows and knees covered by makeshift guards. He stopped in front of me, looked up, gave a disarming smile, and asked in clear English, "Would you tell me about yourself, muzungu?" I did so and asked him his name. "By name I am called William," he replied. Then he invited me to listen to a song he had made up, with the refrain "I would like to know Jesus." Amid the chaos of the marketplace, in a street packed with trucks and bikes and people, among a million different noises and smells, William sang his song, the smile never leaving his face. It was an unforgettable moment.

Young people like William tear down all the walls I put up. His simplicity and humility fly in the face of what the world says is really important: power, beauty, and possessions. Ironically, William already knows Jesus and teaches me of the meek and humble Christ who ultimately stands at right angles to the world. With all of his poor Arua street companions, William creates an opportunity for God to have a cleaner shot at my heart.

There is a place in Arua called the hawker market, where I buy non-perishable goods. There is a woman who always sits in a narrow alley between the street and the market. She is dressed in rags, her eyes cast down, her hand extended in a quiet request for alms. Sometimes, walking through this alley, I have to dodge human feces. I always give her a few shillings and gently fold her hand around what I give. She looks up at me and thanks me. Her eyes are worn out with life—one sees such eyes often among poor women here. *My God, what is it like to spend your life begging in a filthy alley? What kind of existence is that in a world where there is so much wealth?*

Atibuni

"Don't move your head, Father," Atibuni, my Ugandan logistics man, instructed me. We were having dinner together last night; the room was lit by a kerosene lamp, and we had been talking Ugandan politics. He slowly got up, removed one of his sandals, glided over to me, and quickly and skillfully smashed a scorpion that was about three inches above my head and moving south. "Now," he said with serene nonchalance, "where were we?" I gulped as I looked at the dispatched scorpion. I had no idea where we were. *Just pass me another warm beer,* I thought.

Atibuni is one of my dearest friends. He is a good man, a Benjamin, a Nathanael, an emerald that glistens whatever the sight line. He is six-foot-five, as lean and sinewy as a bamboo stalk, and a Ugandan of the Lugbara tribe. He is in his late twenties, but he is much older than his age indicates. He has been employed by JRS for several years and also owns and operates a small retail outlet in Yoro, the Ugandan village adjacent to our compound. He was an orphan early in life and supports himself and a dead sister's six children with this business and his JRS salary. He assumes all of this responsibility with the natural grace of one who does what is to be expected.

A few months ago, his boss at Rhino, Paco, returned to Mexico after an extended illness. JRS asked me to take over as director of the settlement project, so Atibuni and I have been working together. He is my main man, my go-to guy: he helps with shopping, building, sorting out problems, and translating; he offers me tips on ways of proceeding and puts me in touch with important people. Everyone in this region knows him and respects him. And I really love him. He is sensitive and reliable and loyal. And he laughs at all my corny jokes.

Occasionally Providence gives us people who help us make sense of life. Atibuni is that for me. In my first years in Africa, he has been another sun in my life. He casts his clear light when I am lost in cultural darkness, neutralizes the shadows of critical situations, and offers the warmth of his dedication and love. He is a solid guy, steady and enduring. We were friends from the first time we met, and we became closer as we encountered together the challenges of the bush. He is one of God's most wonderful creations.

Naming a Child

All the JRS staff, plus my best catechists—Minga, Tuwanga, Otim, Luaate, and Dudu—and I were having lunch after a morning of planning programs for the next six months, and we started talking about the impending birth of the first child of my staff person Wawa. I asked him if he and his wife had decided on a name for the child, and everyone began laughing. As I subsequently found out, Africans don't name their kids until after the birth, and it is a family affair, not just decided by mom and dad. To ask them what name they will give is as strange and hilarious as asking what they think of the weather tomorrow. As one staffer, a Kenyan, said, "We don't buy the cloth until we see it."

Names are given based on the context of the birth, and the elders lead the way. So my logistics man was given the Lugbara name of Atibuni, which means "born for the grave," because a large number of children in his family had died soon after birth. A child might be given the Arabic name Taban, which means "tired," if the mother is so at birth. Theopista, our cook, was given her name because it means "one who trusts in God," and her father and mother, people of great faith, trusted in God to keep her alive. Sometimes children are given an English name, like Sunday, which reflects the day of the birth. Once I baptized a child named Nelson Mandela, whom the parents admired very much.

Given all of this, I have decided that the name Gary is pretty wooden and unexciting. Perhaps I will change it.

Prayer Reflection

I have lately been aware of the prayer from Psalm 90: "Let us wake in the morning filled with your love." Having just finished Mary Purcell's book on St. Ignatius, *The First Jesuit*, I am even more aware of that plea. I am so far from being filled with God's love when I read about saints. I am aware of my shortcomings, my sin, my loneliness, my distractions, my anger at people, my distance from a passionate love for God, and I wonder at the different interior universes of Ignatius and the mystics compared to mine. I ask for this love. Sometimes I am moved by God's presence, but it never lasts, because I become distracted, like Peter, convinced in the first moment of walking on water and then sinking in disbelief. I would like just once to love God with all the passion with which I love another person whom I know loves me. Ignatius says to stay and relish the consolation of the movement. But, sinking into love and never wanting it to end, I lose my grip on whatever the movement is, figuring that it is just an emotional burst, like a flare on the sun. Here, then gone.

I am contemplating this again tonight and feeling sorry for myself. Maybe it has just been a long, difficult day and I am tired. To bed.

✸

But I woke up. At two a.m.

The sight through my mosquito net was magical. Scores of fireflies were grazing on the grass roof of my tukul. How did they sneak in? They always fill me with joy. Did they know their great admirer was lying beneath them in the darkness, gawking, spellbound? All my preoccupations were obliterated by those tiny blinking beacons in the night.

I am here, guys, I am here. Just look down. I am here.

I fell asleep and was okay.

A Mother's Voice Crying Out in the Wilderness

Atibuni normally greets and interviews individuals when they come to our compound to request aid. There are many. He informed me one morning of a woman who needed to see me. She had come from Yelulu, a small village in the northeastern part of the Rhino Camp Refugee Settlement. She had traveled the nearly ten miles by foot on a brutally hot day.

I ducked under the low entry to the open structure called a pyot where our guests wait, and there I stood face-to-face with a towering woman who was clearly undernourished, wearing a long, faded orange dress, gold earrings, and a headdress that matched her dress. Her face, adorned with high cheekbones, was smooth, unblemished except for three subtle V-shaped lines from her temples to the middle of her forehead: the ritual scars of the Dinka. She was, even in her thin frailty, a beautiful woman. I greeted her in Arabic and asked her name. She responded in English, "By name I am called Rebecca." Her face was strained, a look of concern and fatigue that went much deeper than just tiredness from having walked a great distance. I see this look all the time: it is the look of hunger and poverty.

In her arms, Rebecca held a small child.

I asked her how I could help.

She spoke in Arabic and Atibuni translated: "Father, I am now alone because my husband is fighting with the Liberation Army in Sudan. My child cannot nurse because I cannot produce breast milk. It will soon starve to death if there is no food. Can you help me with money so that I can buy cow's milk?" She addressed me as *Baba*, the affectionate term for "Father."

To make clear the devastating fact of her inability to produce milk, most likely a result of malnutrition, she asked if I would like to see her breasts. Before I could answer, she gently pulled down the top of her dress, cupped her breasts, and held them out for me to see. I was struck at once by the absurdity of it all, and yet the humanity of it all. I stared at her barren breasts, asking myself, *Why is she showing me? I'm not a doctor.*

But perhaps I was, in that moment. She was looking not so much for a diagnosis as for some kind of consolation and assurance—and, of course, financial assistance. Nodding, I gulped and said, "Uh, yeah, Rebecca, they sure look unproductive to me." I have no idea how Atibuni finessed that translation.

Underneath all this, a gloom took hold in my heart. Children are considered to be a blessing from God in this culture—as in most cultures—and the more children one has, the more transparent the blessing. And yet I couldn't help but think, *Isn't it foolish and cruel to continue to have babies when you cannot provide for them?* But I was trying to intellectualize a problem that can't be framed in rational terms. In wartime, one isn't thinking of birth control and family planning. The issue was a plain one: this young mother was about to lose her child because she could not produce milk. It's not hard to understand how she might see this as a reversal of God's blessing.

Near her village, Rebecca could buy cow's milk sold in a Pepsi bottle for around four hundred shillings, about twenty-five cents. I gave her enough for a month's supply and told her to come back when she needed more.

As she left, she grasped my hand, thanked me, and told me, "Chol is your child now, and as he lives he will pass your generosity on to others." I was knocked out by her wonderful understanding of the interconnectedness of people. I thought, too, that it reflected a true grasp of the notion of the body of Christ.

> A man never hates his own body, but he feeds it and looks after it; and that is the way Christ treats the Church, because it is his body—and we are its living parts. (Ephesians 5:29–30)

As she was leaving, I asked her what full name she had given to her son. "Jacob Chol," she answered. She explained that the Dinka word *chol* means "the child who was born after the one who died." So I knew what happened to Rebecca's first child: he perished because he had no breast milk. All that his little sucking mouth could find was a warm breast over his mother's warm heart. Rebecca told me about her first child with strength, her face disclosing neither pain nor anger. She said then, "God is good," marrying two difficult realities: that Chol's brother had died and that everything is given and taken away by God. Not an easy connection to make, perhaps impossible for those of us who take food and decent medical care for granted.

It is always hard for me to stack bush theology up against my own. But in the end, the person of faith, like Job, offers this: *The Lord gives and the Lord takes away.* This belief reflects an acceptance of crushing conditions, no matter how severe. Yet it is about not only accepting what cannot be changed, but also offering up adversity to the benevolent God. I see this attitude every day in the people here, but I myself am not very good at it.

I encountered Rebecca and Chol at different times after our first meeting. At the marketplace in Arua, she came over to me with a few Dinka women, greeted me, placed her little Chol in my arms, and stood back to admire the two of us, drooling Chol and Baba Gary, staring at each other. When there is an opportunity, Rebecca wants her son to be held by his father.

A Paratrooper in a Diaper

The sight of blood finally snapped me out of my stubbornness.
I was sitting in the latrine at three in the morning, my flashlight flickering on the floor. Lizards were hanging out on the walls, thumb-sized cockroaches were scurrying above and below me, and bats were rustling in the space between the wooden rafters and the tin roof. But they didn't scare me. The blood scared me. *My* blood. In my shorts. This was not your basic diarrhea. This was serious.

A few days earlier, my staff and I had gone shopping in Arua. It was a dry-season day on the equator, the temperature topping out at 110. By the time we arrived home—after a ninety-minute drive on dirt roads—we were sticky with sweat and covered in dust. In my case, there were other inconveniences: a pounding headache and an aching body. Then, as I was taking a quick cool shower, a tremor moved through me, and my stomach clenched up. As the afternoon progressed, the symptoms got worse. It looked like malaria: headache, chills, fever, nausea, general body fatigue. I started popping malaria medicine, a treatment of four pills a day for five days.

That was my first mistake.

The chills eventually ceased, and I thought the whole episode would blow over. In the tropics, these things happen: a glass of bad water here, a little fungus there; now an insect bite, then an allergic reaction. I thought I knew what I was up against. I woke in the middle of the night, poured myself a glass of fruit juice, and sat down at my desk, thinking,

Hey, I don't feel too bad. I just can't sleep. Then I threw up: juice, eggs, whatever else had gone in since lunch. Soon, I was back in the latrine. The sickness didn't let up for three days.

The JRS staff checked in on me periodically, but I waved them away. I thought it was malaria and that I would be back to normal in a few days.

Sitting in the latrine on the morning of the fourth day, I knew something else was going on. I hadn't been able to eat for days, and my stomach had expelled everything in it, but still I was sick. I remembered a story a veteran coworker on the streets of Portland had once told me about a sign at the desk in one of the skid row hotels in the 1970s. It was a list of names, and above the names it said, *The following list of people cannot stay here, because they shit on the floor.* I thought to myself, *Better put my name on the list, guys.* I started to laugh at the thought of it—and then to worry that I was losing my mind.

In this dark, out-of-control moment, I wandered into a prayer that went something like this: *I am here in this land, in this obscure place, because my deepest heart followed all the signs of invitation that you gave. I trust you and that you want me to get better. So I am in your hands now.*

Five minutes later, the decision came to me: *I must attend to this business. Now.* This wasn't malaria, and I was a fool to tough it out on my own. I needed help.

I left the latrine and went over to Atibuni's tukul. It was four o'clock in the morning. I told him to get our driver, because we would be leaving for the Arua airstrip at sunrise, ultimately heading for Kampala, 350 miles south. A doctor there had treated me for other tropical ailments.

Victor, our driver, came in at dawn. Before leaving, anticipating an accident along the way, I rigged up a towel diaper, fastened with safety pins. It was so outrageously bulky that I could not button up my Levi's, which I masked with a long jacket. January is a scorcher in Uganda, so I probably looked pretty silly. But I didn't care. I collapsed in the backseat as we took off for Arua.

By the time I arrived in Kampala, I was whipped, thanks to the dehydration, the loss of blood, and the lack of food and sleep. But, blessedly, I'd had no accidents.

The superior general of the Jesuits, Peter-Hans Kolvenbach, is alleged to have said that the Jesuits in JRS are the paratroopers of the society. I thought of that glorious and provocative line as I waddled through Entebbe Airport, my makeshift diaper in place: *Here I am, a paratrooper in a diaper.* Actually, given what I know of my Jesuit friends and their wounded hearts, a paratrooper in a diaper is an appropriate metaphor for many of us in the Society of Jesus.

I was in the doctor's office within two hours. Old Doc Stokely, an English expatriate who runs a tropical disease clinic in Kampala, made a quick diagnosis: dysentery. A couple of doses of antibiotics and a few hours later, I began to feel better.

That night, I fell asleep early. I woke before dawn. All was still. Off in the distance, I could hear the bells of one of the nearby Catholic churches calling people for an early Mass. I lay in my bed at the Jesuit residence in Kampala, but my soul knelt. I was okay. My god, I was okay. I got out of bed and stood staring into the darkness of my room, flashing on the events of the past several days. I was restless but at peace, sensing the presence of God and how all the jagged edges of the past several days had been smoothed and sealed. I was like a rescued miner emerging from the darkness after a cave-in, coming up and out into the day, waving to the world and breathing deeply, weary but happy. I returned to my bed and whispered a prayer of gratitude.

I am always struck by the fact that I can embrace faith in hopeless situations. It is a paradoxical idea. But in those moments when my life is unraveling, I am touched by the truth that I am in God's hands. No matter how dark the circumstances, God is in them, for God is the benevolent and solicitous ground beneath me. So I am steadied, even consoled. I make my comebacks.

I cannot feel sorry for myself when every day I meet people who struggle with disease and death. They are as much a part of the East African reality as the sun and the rain. When I joined JRS, I never thought that my accompanying the refugees would include suffering from afflictions that they endure constantly. But in those afflictions, I encounter God. It is a sort of mystical experience: even here, and maybe especially here, I meet God. However intense my moaning and groaning, the moment of confrontation puts things in perspective. God's love for me trumps the chaos that invades my life. The truth that I am loved and desired rings in me like those clear and pure predawn church bells in Kampala.

Letter from Arua

Dear S.,

I write this from Arua, where I have come for a meeting and have the night free. I miss you so much. Each morning I pray in gratitude for my knowledge of you and that you have stuck with me throughout my stay here. You are a wonderful friend.

You asked in your last letter about the contrasts in my life. I struggle with the complex culture here, yet I always feel welcome. I laugh a lot and have moments of flat-out terror. Regarding the latter, I recently encountered a cobra in the shower stall on our compound; it was cooling off in a corner. I hit its hooded head with a bucket, slammed the door against it, and then beat the stunned thing to death. When it was over, I stood there buck naked alternately laughing and crying.

I spend my days responding to endless and frequently impossible requests and adjusting to the nuances and defects of staff and of those employed by other nongovernmental organizations. Little things can make the most emotionally depleting day manageable: a cold beer, a letter that tells me I am loved, a crackling strain of classical music over BBC shortwave, a breeze sneaking in under the heat, a child unaccountably holding on to my hand from the moment I got out of the truck until it was time for me to leave the village. Little things.

Our JRS project continues to march forward on a number of fronts, cobras notwithstanding. We have now enrolled hundreds of adults in adult-ed classes, which take place outside on rows of logs. We also give money to groups of eight or more who launch an income-generating operation that has promise of success: for instance, selling grain purchased in Arua at the local markets in the settlement, or buying second-hand clothes, fixing them up, and selling them. The groups eventually pay the loan back through profits. We also lead seminars at each chapel for leaders and their people, usually around theological matters. And, of course, I celebrate the Eucharist in the settlement villages.

I was recently here in Arua for three days to attend a seminar for catechists and for follow-up blood tests at the clinic (malaria caught up with me in April—more on that later). Catechists run the show in the settlement in many respects, attending to the prayers of the community when there is no Eucharist, emphasizing Scripture, and helping the people apply the Gospel to their lives. There are some excellent catechists in the settlement who are powerful in their preaching. In this diocese, they do 95 percent of the funerals, and there are a lot of funerals. Most of the catechists tend to be men in their thirties and forties, and a large number have been trained in Arua at the primary diocesan center in the North, or at another center in Yumbe, west of the Nile and close to the Sudan border.

The program participants must have a secondary education and a sacramental marriage and be able to read, write, and speak English (because of the many languages in the settlement, the training centers must operate in a common tongue). The course work takes a year, requiring significant time away from home. When an individual is away at the training, the home village and the JRS project attend to the needs of the person's family. The financing for participants comes in part from diocesan grants (money given by philanthropic foundations in Europe) and in part from the home parish of the catechist. They are trained in Scripture, church history, catechesis, preaching techniques, liturgy, social awareness, and spirituality. I have come to love and respect the catechists, men like Minga, Asega, Kenyi, Tuwanga, Otim, Luaate, and Lokuri. And I am in the hunt for more women to take on the role.

The rains have been poor; one often hears the dreaded word: *drought*. There is so much hunger as it is. I always knew how to get food to homeless street people in the States; here there is no food and no money. It is painful to hear parents say that their children have not eaten in two or three days. Is that the word? *Painful*? It's deeper than pain. Without food, the people are susceptible to what I call hunger diseases, diseases that strike when the body's defenses are weakened by malnutrition. I have lingering guilt when I eat and know that many of the brothers and sisters will face the day without food.

Speaking of disease, I was finally nailed by malaria—the prospect was always there, lurking, only a matter of when and where. It was a hurricane that breached my shoreline swiftly, powerfully, and mercilessly. It started as a bad headache, and before I knew what hit me I was dealing with a stomach disorder, aching muscles, teeth-chattering chills, lots of sweating, and a high temperature. I was a mess. I have never felt so rotten in my life. The medication worked, but between it and the malaria, I was left feeling edgy and emotionally blunted and vulnerable. I know you worried about this, but I am better now, and my body's immune system will be more prepared the next time a hungry mosquito injects its parasites into my bloodstream.

Of many things: women carrying twenty-liter cans of water on their heads; the smell of rain on the wind before it reaches our compound; dogs underneath the altar at Mass; teak tree leaves the size of small sails; rejoicing with a young man on the arrival of his wife from Sudan after two years of separation; Mary and Mary, two orphaned teenagers, very happy when I bought them two kilos of rice; dawns sung into existence by doves and cuckoo birds; the distant six a.m. jet heading north toward Addis Ababa; the intoxicating juice of a mango, leaking and smeared all over my face and hands; snails the size of softballs lazily making their way across the road; encounters with African men and women so guileless they seem to be from another planet—a planet of good hearts. God, I love this place.

I pray for truth and happiness in your life and your marriage, and for your parents.

My regards to all,

Gary

Cause of Death: Life

The leadership of the village of Ngurua, where I celebrated the Eucharist one Sunday morning, requested that I come to the residence of a young man whose wife had died the night before. After Mass, we moved through the camp of small tukuls. It is an extremely poor village, even among the other poor villages of Rhino. I walked in the middle of a long line of people, many of whom had been at Mass; others who had not attended were aware of what was happening and had joined the procession. Grief is a communal experience in a tribe, made more so by the close quarters in which people live in the settlement villages, and though they mind their own business when it comes to the intimate matters of family, all know what is going on with their neighbor. And, too, the history of flight and suffering and death is shared by all.

The silent line moved over dusty footpaths, only the occasional cry of a child or bark of a dog interrupting. Even the very young children joined us, as well as most of the teenagers. We came to the compound of the deceased, and I was met by the husband. He was young, in his early twenties, and the strain of the last few days was apparent on his face. He took my hand and led me to his dead wife. I stooped beneath the small opening of the one-room tukul and entered into the smell of death and dirt and defeat. The tukul was full of women, seated on the dirt floor in a silent circle of mourning around the dead woman, who lay wrapped in a blanket, her young head visible. They all turned to look at me, and I greeted each one with a handshake.

The young wife had died the night before, at twenty-two years old, due to complications from the birth of her second child a week before. As far as I could figure out through the translation of the husband's words, she had hemorrhaged to death, and the midwives, for all their experience, could not stop the bleeding.

The women parted, making a spot for me to kneel before the body. Standing behind me were the leaders of the chapel, who were not much older than this woman. They had been in this place so many times before, veterans of the premature deaths of mothers and children that are common here. I knelt and prayed, but it was a distracted prayer, because I was thinking about the husband and his needs, and how in the world he was going to feed the newborn.

As I left the tukul, I stopped and talked with the father. He held the week-old baby, deprived in the long term of a mother and in the short term of a mother's warmth and milk. The father showed me the freshly dug grave, adjacent to their tukul, where his wife would be buried later that day. He asked if I could help with another blanket, since his wife would be buried in the only one they possessed, and if I could give him a few shillings for cow's milk. They don't have formula here; it is the stuff of another solar system.

At some point, as I was walking out of the compound, my arm around the shoulder of this young man, I lost it, drawing away momentarily to weep in that obscure little place that was baking in grief and heat. These moments are always a blow to the gut for me, and all I can do in the face of the overwhelming odds confronting the refugee is mourn. It is such madness, the death of a young person. Today in particular was difficult, because it was my birthday. What tragic irony: I celebrated my birthday on the day I prayed over the dead body of a sister who was forty years younger than me.

Otim, the local catechist and a good friend, told me that he would do the funeral later in the day. Would this not remind him, I asked, of another day last year when he buried his own five-year-old daughter, struck down by malaria? "Yes," he said. "But Abuna, we are in God's hands."

To say that this mother died of complications from childbirth is to dance around the real issue. She died of malnutrition and a compromised immune system that broke down in a fight against postnatal infection. It was no contest. When I see the gaunt bodies that attend to these moments; when I consider that even the most basic resources—proper health care, clean water, decent housing—are not available to this long-suffering people; when, in a word, I see a life riddled with deprivations, I have to conclude that the cause of this death was life.

In my mind's eye, I see the millions of refugees of the world, spawned by the decisions of political power brokers. These decision makers seem to be indifferent to the suffering they cause, a suffering that crashes down on the heads of ordinary people who only want to raise a family, grow food for their kids, and sleep peaceably at night. And beyond the people who cause war and nurture their own death-dealing agendas, there are the people in wealthy developed cultures who have learned to compartmentalize the poor of the world into a problem "out there": a global version of out of sight, out of mind.

Letter from Mwanza, Tanzania

Dear B.,

Hi. I write this at the southern tip of Lake Victoria in Tanzania, where I am attending a meeting of pastoral agents in JRS Eastern Africa countries: Uganda, Sudan, Tanzania, Kenya, and Ethiopia. It has been an opportunity to stand back and assess things, which I needed to do as I head into the homestretch of my time in Rhino. In the evening, we dine at a little village restaurant on the beach and have some delicious tilapia.

I have reflected on what I have been doing and will try to answer your question about my work.

For the past several months, my staff and I have been organizing and conducting a series of one-day and three-day seminars for our refugee church leadership: catechists; people involved in the care of the sick and aged; youth, women, and liturgical leaders; chapel chairpersons; facilitators of Small Christian Communities (gatherings of people in the villages who meet regularly to read and study Scripture); and those developing small businesses. In general, we have realized our goals, and the next four months will be a time of much pastoral work within the villages and follow-up on the seminars.

We hold the three-day seminars at the training facility located three miles from the JRS compound. Actually, "training facility" is perhaps a bit elaborate: it consists of one classroom, a latrine, a small kitchen for open-fire cooking, a storage room, and a couple of outdoor benches that we use for group discussions. The seminars are humbling. There are many challenges: language issues (determining which one to use and arranging for translators), illiteracy, sickness (malaria hits two or three people at every seminar), lack of electricity, crying babies (who come with their moms), the long distances to the facility from people's home villages, rain and heat, lack of running water, insects and poisonous reptiles, simple food (beans and flour and a little cabbage and dried fish), sleeping arrangements in the seminar room (we have to partition off the room since men and women both attend), and a few thousand other things. The logistics of such seminars are daunting, but fortunately my staff is smart and well organized. "That's why I pay you guys the big bucks," I joke with them.

Our ministry involves more than just organizing seminars and teaching theology, of course. I also have a lot of one-on-one meetings with people in the settlements. Tuesdays are difficult, because that is when I see the many people who come to us for assistance. One of the last people I saw last week wanted money to purchase sugar and tea for the large gathering of people who would come to mourn a death in his family. I had been giving out assistance all day and was becoming irritable, mildly put off by so many wanting money or supplies.

The man standing before me was in his mid- to late twenties, thin, sad. He had a strong handshake and the coarse skin of a person who has worked in hard labor all his life. He came to us for supplies for the funeral of his nine-month-old daughter, Viola, who died of pneumonia complicated by a severe case of malaria. I informed him, in one of my more arrogant comments as JRS project director, that we could not take financial responsibility for every funeral. I shall never forget the look of bewilderment on his face, bringing into stark relief the small-mindedness of my comment.

I stopped myself, my heart impaled by his look. I asked him if she was his only child.

He said, "No, this is the fourth child."

"And the others?" I asked.

"Dead also, Father, all in the first year of their lives. I myself and my wife are nearly dying with grief."

It was a direct hit. The rubble of my arrogance was scattered everywhere. Feeling like the consummate jerk, I mumbled something about how sorry I was. Imagine: four children. Dead. His own. His all. The horror of it.

I turned to Atibuni, who was translating. "Give him anything he needs."

The young man shook my hand again with his leathery hands. He thanked me and was gone with Atibuni.

Things like this happen here. I am learning.

Please don't worry about me so much; what is important is that you pray for me and for my people here. God has the ultimate hand in everything. I hear the drums of death nearly every week, part of the mourning and burial ritual of native Ugandans. The drumming can last for three days and nights. But even surrounded by death, I am reminded of the wealth of life.

And there is abundant new life. Recently, two midwives from a nearby village came to ask if I could take Mary, a young orphan woman I know and love, to a clinic; she had gone into labor with her first child. I drove for two hours over bad roads looking for an open clinic, with Mary and the two faithful midwives in the backseat. Bumping along, nervously looking over my shoulder at the hard-breathing mother-to-be, whose contractions were coming at shorter intervals, I tried to say something in Arabic to support her, but I was nervous and all I could manage was "Have a nice day." I was prepared for a backseat delivery, but we made it to an open clinic, and shortly after we arrived the baby was born. A boy. Mary named him Gary, because of my involvement in the delivery. My name sounds kind of goofy next to the Sudanese surname (Ondoa), but who cares. So now, as far as I know, there is one Gary in a settlement of thirty-five thousand. Not too long ago, a mother came to me shortly after she had given birth to a daughter, on the day I said Mass in her village. She asked the name of my deceased mother. So somewhere in the villages is a young girl named Eunice.

More life in abundance: about two weeks ago, a gift duck (from the mothers in a village where I baptized a dozen kids) hatched—count them—thirteen ducklings in our compound. Oh, the sight of that mother duck majestically strolling out of the nesting area, her fluffy, peeping, black and yellow little guys in tow. I stood gawking, the whole scene a light in the darkness. I, Mr. City Boy, was the most excited out of the whole staff. It is no big deal to Africans—they've been there, done that. If there had been cigars, I would have passed them around.

I love you and miss you.

Gary

Journal: September 2002

Anointing and Being Anointed

Last Sunday, I celebrated Mass in the village of Tika. Walking into the chapel, led by the young Kizito dancers, I am always knocked out by the music, the singing, and the scores of people swaying in unison. But on that Sunday, I was moved to tears. I am not sure why. Was it the beauty of the music? The raw contrast between the impoverished little chapel and the glittering Western churches I have seen? The faces of everyone turned toward me, smiling and welcoming?

There was a baptismal liturgy in the middle of the Eucharistic celebration. The fifty-three children were from the six Tika villages and had been prepared by the local catechists. After a question-and-answer homily, built on a youth-performed drama from the Gospel, the congregation moved outside, gathering underneath an enormous mahogany tree for the baptisms. I was surrounded by concentric circles of mothers and babies, fathers and sponsors, the Kizito, the talented musicians and the throbbing choir, other members of the community, and half a dozen chickens and two sleepy-eyed, emaciated dogs. Moving down the line of children during the anointing, I came upon one frail malarial baby, Genty, with beads of sweat on her tiny forehead. I knew she would die soon. Her mouth was listlessly wrapped around her mother's nipple. The mother, for her part, tried to muster a smile for me. For the few seconds my fingers were on Genty's head, images of all the sick children and sick adults I have encountered in the settlement hovered just inside the frontiers of my consciousness, a dark reservoir that I kept pushing back. The suffering and death in the refugee villages can break a person. I moved on to the next child, my eyes clouding over.

When the liturgy was finished, there was enthusiastic applause; the women ululated in celebration, and the church moved forward. I myself was anointed by the sanctity of the good hearts surrounding me. In that moment, I was experiencing the body of Christ. I whispered a silent prayer, asking God for peace in the world and a life of peace for those dear children. We processed back to the chapel and finished the Mass. Morning became afternoon. Hours after we began, I was eating beans and drinking tea and bantering with the leaders of the chapel.

I spent half an hour before leaving Tika playing with a yo-yo that I had asked my sister to send. The children were spellbound by it; they crowded in, eager to touch me and to figure out how on earth I made the darn thing stay spinning at the end of the string.

I learned two days later that Genty had died. She was her mother's second child to perish.

Baptism for a Deaf Child

Before Mass today at the Simbili chapel, the catechist, Isaac, and a woman from the village brought a twelve-year-old orphan boy, the woman's nephew, to me. They wanted to discuss whether he was ready for baptism. The boy was deaf. I was told that he was able to make the sign of the cross and that he attended Prayers and Mass with the family. I asked Isaac and the aunt what they thought; after all, they knew him best. They said yes, he is ready. I turned to the boy and asked him what he wanted to do. Isaac translated my question for the aunt, who in turn repeated it in a crude sign language for the boy. He beamed and nodded. I added that they should teach in his presence, let him watch the other kids and the praying community, and trust that God will make up the difference.

It is a hard and long road for disabled refugee children, who face added hardship on an already difficult path. In this boy's case, he has to live with the belief of many of his people that deafness is God's curse—a belief fueled by witch doctors. What I would give to be able to reach out, put my hands on his ears, and heal him. (Indeed, what *would* I give?) I will baptize him the next time I am at Simbili for Mass; I will have the people in the congregation come up after the baptism and impose their hands on his head and ears. It will be a sign from the Christian community that he is not alone in his silence.

They Sang All the Way

At Ocea, three of the catechists, Lokuri, Luaate, and Dudu, conducted a four-day seminar for women, facilitated primarily by Dudu, a trained woman catechist, and Sister Gloria, a nun from Arua. Gloria directs a school for women that helps them develop community projects and become self-reliant. The purpose of the seminar was to give the women a deeper understanding of the church, its various talents, and the necessity of women leadership. Gloria also spent time talking about income-generating opportunities and how they might be accomplished. It was a gathering, too, that was geared toward affirming the women not only as leaders but also as women. Two representatives from each of the nineteen chapels in the settlement attended the seminar. Many of them brought their babies and younger daughters or sons who were old enough to babysit. In the end, we had almost sixty people to feed and house. The women love these events where they can come together.

A standout was Anite, a graceful mother of five. Her husband is working in Congo, and she is a smart servant of her family and the community. She acted as an unofficial leader in the seminar, affirming the women and asking questions that needed to be addressed: What are the economic conditions of refugee women? What are their options? How can they be empowered? She helped the facilitators lead discussions around these questions, cajoling the women to talk and cracking them up when they needed a break from the serious conversation. (I suspect that men took a benevolent beating in those moments.) Anite has been a good friend to me and has helped me understand her culture better.

As I watched the women in the seminar gather strength from one another, it helped me understand the universal church. It should be a community that is compassionate, offering companionship to and living in solidarity with the least of our brothers and sisters. Caring African women, especially as they tend to AIDS victims, provide an image of that church and can help us better understand what we are called to be.

On the final day of the seminar, we had Mass, and then the two eldest women slowly moved around the circle and imposed their hands on the heads of their sisters, sending them back to their villages with a mission. The elder women even came to the back of the room and blessed me. After lunch, all the women from the east side of the settlement climbed into the JRS pickup, and we took off for their villages. Victor, the JRS driver, took the women from the west side home in another pickup.

Driving a group anywhere here is an extraordinary experience. Everyone starts singing, and the longer the trip, the louder it gets. Usually one person sings verses and all join in on the refrain. As we approached each village, all the women in the truck would incorporate the village name into the song. At each stop, the villagers would come out to greet us—and *they* would start singing and clapping as they welcomed their two sisters home. This happened at every village; the women sang *all the way*. And me? I was like a little kid who had snuck into the biggest, hottest movie in town and got to see it all for free. When we got to the final village, Odobu, the last two women were sitting in the backseat singing like canaries. I let the first off at the entrance to the village, and the one who remained, my buddy Regina, kept right on rolling with a Congolese song. Finally, we reached her home, and as she was getting out of the truck, she gave me a wonderful smile, revealing the truth of her happy heart with her eyes, and then bade me farewell in Arabic. What a trip. What an unbelievable trip.

Lillian

Yesterday I had lunch with Lillian, a young Ugandan woman who helps us with work in the compound. I told her that I would be leaving Rhino Camp soon for another assignment, and in her sadness over my departure, she said that she would like to give me a gift when the time comes. We have become very close over the years. She said, "I will give you a goat." It is one of the best gifts a person can give. It is a gift of great cost, but, more important, it is a means of sustenance and a symbol of life.

I was moved by her simple focus on the gift, oblivious to the realities of my meatless diet and travel restrictions. We talked into the afternoon; she told me that no man had ever treated her with such respect and care as I had. It was one of those unguarded moments that I have rarely experienced with a woman in this culture. She is one I will miss very much.

The next day, she brought me an alternate gift, an ebony carving of a giraffe. It remains one of my most precious possessions.

Letter from Rhino Camp
Refugee Settlement

Dear D.,

I wanted to get this off to you, as I will be leaving the Rhino Camp settlement soon for another assignment. My last moments with two of my catechists were very special, and I must share them with you.

My final Eucharist in the settlement was in a village called Olujobo. There was more singing and dancing than usual, because the people know it will be a long time before I return, if I ever return. On my way back to the JRS compound, I gave the catechists Luaate and Asega a ride to their home village, Wanyange. They had walked nearly five miles to participate in the Mass.

When we arrived at their home, we stepped out of the pickup in the center of the village, and they both embraced me. This was probably the last time we would see each other. It is the dry season, and red dust blew into our faces. The village was alive with chickens and goats and people. Barefoot children surrounded the pickup with big smiles, curious about the *cawaja abuna* (the "white father"). The villagers approached us, greeting and welcoming back their two sons and me.

In another world, where civil war might not have disrupted their lives, Luaate and Asega could have been physicians or lawyers or priests or university professors or businessmen. Both are young, smart, fluent in several languages, and deeply religious; they are two of my best catechists. Luaate, the older of the two, is thirty-one and the father of three.

Six years ago, he gathered his wife, his children, and his elderly mother and fled the hostilities in Southern Sudan.

In the barrenness of the Wanyange village, he held me at arm's length and looked at me intently through his beat-up rimless glasses. His words were clear and direct in his impeccable English: "We will carry on, and the African church will go forward; you have been a great gift to us. Your presence is a testimony that the world has not forgotten us." It was a moment to die for, and to live by. I see on the faces of Luaate and Asega the very dignity and courage that led me to fall in love with the Sudanese refugees; they are a people of unpretentious goodness, enduring faith, and unyielding hope.

As I was heading back to the JRS compound, reflecting on those embraces and the bittersweet final liturgy in Olujobo, I thought of what the people I have served here have taught me. I have learned a simple and strong trust in God in a place where everything can and often does go wrong, where poverty and malnutrition are part of every life, and where life is at best fragile and uncertain. The people here have taught me that in Africa, for all its grinding poverty, for all its death, for all its Amins and Konys, the inner force of the human spirit endures. I have discovered that in their faith, the refugees embrace the church in spite of its weaknesses and warts, and that the church finds its meaning and purpose in Christ's fundamental message: that human beings are made in the image of God, and that the least of our brothers and sisters are to be the focus of the best expressions of the church's love. It is among people like Luaate and Asega that I see more clearly the size and power of the mandate of the Society of Jesus: to be with the poor. They are to be our preferential option, and they hold the key to our understanding of who we are as Jesuits and what we can become.

My health is good, to respond to your inquiries. There are always a few nicks here and there, but in general I will conclude this part of my time here in fairly good health.

I hope you are doing better healthwise. Life is so beautiful. And so fragile.

Love,

Gary

Everything

I have had a chance to return to the States for a break. It has been good to get out of the river and dry off for a while—and, too, to hold in my arms once again the people I love.

One of those people is Pauli. She lived next door to me when I was going to high school in California's Central Valley and has always been like a second mother to me. She is now in her nineties. She has shrunk—her word—in the march of years, but she still has radiant eyes and a quick mind and a self-deprecatory sense of humor. She laughs easily, always has. She was widowed in the eighties, and her daughter and son died prematurely.

I went to visit Pauli, and we talked over an afternoon at her apartment. We shared our lives, mine in Africa and hers in the assisted care facility where she now lives. At one point, I asked her about her relationship with Tony, her husband, to whom she was married for fifty-three years.

As she spoke steadily about Tony, her commitment to him opened before me, slowly disclosing the tenderness and fragility of her love, like the first rains after the dry season gradually uncover the green beauty of Uganda. I knew Tony and loved him very much, but this was the first time I had asked her to speak about her love for him. At a certain point in the marriage, she simply surrendered to love, and it was incarnated in her care for him and the kids.

"And what do you miss most about him?" I asked.

Without hesitation and with a face full of splendid love, she responded, "Oh Gary, everything."

Everything. For her, it was a word that moved in two directions: all that he was, she loved; and all that she had to give, she gave. Everything.

We embraced and I left. Pauli's totality of love swept over me, juxtaposed with the American culture to which I have returned briefly, with its celebration of superficiality and empty allurement, with its snorting condescension toward self-denial. That the continent of Africa chronically suffers from poverty, illiteracy, malnutrition, war, corrupt and oppressive governments, and one million babies a year dead to malaria is lost on us. It's another commercial on TV to mute.

Pauli's kind of love, her kind of selflessness, is alien in a culture that is rotting in self-absorption. But her "everything" makes sense to me. In its purity and clarity, it rings in the deepest part of me. It echoes God's love of the beloved—all God's creatures—and it echoes the completeness of Christ's giving: his life, his death. As I pulled away from Pauli's apartment building, I wanted her "everything" to be a mantra for me, helping me see the refugees and the poor as God sees them, and helping me love them and surrender my heart to them as Christ did.

Part 2

Adjumani Refugee Settlement

Letter from Adjumani Refugee Settlement

Dear D. and D.,

I write this from Adjumani, in northern Uganda, a radar blip on the map with a population of maybe six thousand. It is twenty-five miles south of the Sudan border and ten miles east of the Nile River. The JRS project here encompasses two major activities: education and pastoral care. We operate in two refugee settlements: the Adjumani Refugee Settlement, composed of thirty villages containing sixty thousand people, and the Palorinya Refugee Settlement, on the west side of the Nile, composed of twenty-one villages and containing about thirty-five thousand people.

In partnership with the UNHCR, the JRS projects in the Adjumani and Palorinya settlements run dozens of nursery schools, more than sixty primary schools, and five secondary schools and sponsor a large number of secondary school graduates who have gone on to the Ugandan equivalent of a junior college. JRS pays the salaries of the top administration in the project, and the UNHCR pays all the teachers and the program expenses. There are about forty Sudanese and Ugandan JRS employees working on the education efforts in the main office, in the town of Adjumani. They are good men and women who don't make much money but are dedicated to educating young refugees in preparation for their return to Sudan.

I direct the pastoral arm of the whole enterprise. My work involves supporting the local Catholic Church, which ministers to refugees—Catholic and non-Catholic—in the Adjumani and Palorinya settlements.

My pastoral team in Adjumani is made up of two Ugandan priests of an indigenous African congregation called the Apostles of Jesus and a Ugandan nun from an African congregation called the Sisters of the Sacred Heart—all three have been assigned to the settlement by the local diocese. In the Palorinya settlement, I also work in conjunction with the local Ugandan Catholic Church, but it can put very few resources into refugee work, because its primary responsibility is to Ugandan Catholics. I am in the villages most of the time, and every weekend I celebrate Mass in a chapel in the Adjumani settlement.

I travel a lot with a driver named Ratib, a Ugandan Madi who knows the roads well. He is a wonderful traveling companion who teaches me new things wherever we go. His quick and practical mind comes in handy when we are faced with the unexpected, as we often are. Plus, he has a great laughing way about him that gets us through all doors. Ratib is a good and resourceful man. He has a wonderful wife and two charming and affectionate little girls who love their *baba*.

The drive to several of the villages in the Palorinya settlement from my home base in Adjumani is about two hours one way, depending on the efficiency of the Nile ferry. It takes about fifteen minutes to cross the Nile, but adherence to schedules is not a strength of the Ugandan department of transportation. Any number of problems can cause delays: engine troubles, propellers jammed by hyacinth, fuel shortages, trucks getting stuck pulling onto or off the ferry, security issues, thunderstorms, and intoxicated personnel. Once we had to wait for a battalion of the Sudan People's Liberation Army (SPLA) to make its way across, taking a shortcut to a base in Southern Sudan. Riding the ferry is an exercise in patience and an adventure into the unknown.

In the compound, I live with three other JRS International staff. We live on the edge of the town of Adjumani, which is home primarily to Ugandans of the Madi tribe. The environment is rich in sights and sounds and smells. Walking in the village, I hear the children call in Madi, "Mundu, Mundu," which means "white man." Their calls are usually accompanied by big grins and big stares. Some kids will flee from my frightening white face, and others will run up to me and grab my hand, as if to say, "You rock, Mundu." In these walks, I dodge pigs, cows, goats, chickens, and turkeys (is there anything uglier than a tom?) in the hunt for food—apparently they return to their owners at night. There is much cultivation here: sweet potatoes, pumpkins, squash, string beans, tomatoes, onions, maize, sorghum, mangoes, jackfruit, watermelons, guavas, and papayas. Everywhere are trees: neem, acacia, mahogany, teak, and jacaranda. At night, as you may imagine in a place where there are no urban lights, the sky is clear, an ocean of stars.

In general, things are good. The adjustment to Adjumani has been easier than the adjustment to Rhino Camp, and that can be attributed to experience. But I am dealing on different turf here and have more challenging responsibilities. I pray a lot.

If ever I am tempted to feel like the high-and-mighty Jesuit from afar, something comes along to humble me. Recently, at my big moment of speaking to all the Adjumani catechists, a frightened lizard dropped onto the table in front of me. My reaction was to stumble back in fear. It reminded me of an episode during my community organizing days in East Oakland when a rat barged across the floor, heading in my direction, during a meeting I was facilitating. Or the time in Rhino when two lizards, blissfully locked in sexual encounter, fell from the ceiling onto my *head* and bounced onto the floor. The catechists in Adjumani, all veterans of encounters with lizards, had a good but sympathetic laugh at my jumpiness. I miss you. Dante wrote somewhere that leaving behind loved ones is the first shaft that the bow of exile shoots. True.

Love,

Gary

Standing Naked before an Angel

It was a Sunday night, about ten o'clock. I was on a bumpy ambulance ride through Kampala, heading for Case Clinic, where I was to have an emergency surgery. An hour earlier, the ever-cool Dr. Stokely, who had treated me for dysentery a couple of years ago, had made the diagnosis, after questioning me about my stomach pain and probing my abdomen. "This is an appendix. And it has to come out. *Now.*"

I had arrived in Kampala that afternoon; on Monday, I was to lead the JRS Eastern Africa country directors in a Day of Reflection, in which they would have time to consider in silence and to share in groups some of the Ignatian spiritual principles underlying their work. The pain in my stomach had started Saturday morning in Adjumani. By the time I arrived at Xavier House, the Jesuit residence in Kampala, it was clear that I wasn't just having stomach cramps. Plans for the next day were put on hold, and Aden, the JRS director for Uganda and Southern Sudan, took me to the clinic.

Guiney, the director of JRS Eastern Africa, who was in town for the Day of Reflection, rode with me in the ambulance, steadying me as I wrenched with every bump in the road. Aden was tailing us in the JRS car. When we arrived at the clinic, I was placed in a wheelchair and wheeled in. I was in a whiteout of pain.

Inside it was dark, quiet. I was taken to a room and laid down. A personable Dr. Abote—chiseled black face, eyes full of heart, around fifty years old—arrived. He called me Gary and told me calmly that they were setting up the operating room. An IV was inserted, and I was led down the hallway to a small room, where a little nurse helped me undress. I towered over her.

"Who are you?" I asked.

"I am called Angel," she replied, her eyes smiling and tender.

I stood naked before an angel. I slipped into one of those ridiculous hospital gowns that are made for elves.

By eleven, I was on my back in the operating theater, Abote standing off to one side, listening to a tape on his Walkman and nodding to me. I wondered what he was listening to. I thought it would be nice to hear some Ravel or Debussy, but in that crisis a blazing refrain from the Rolling Stones would have been more appropriate. A huge anesthesiologist, smiling at me upside down, told me he was about to administer anesthesia. He peered down at me like a bombardier looking down his sights. He lined up for the drop. Bombs away.

Four hours later, the appendix was out. Abote later told me that mine was the longest appendix he had ever seen; I think he said, too, that it was rotten. I was cut from stomach to kidney in an effort to find the migrating appendix and clean up the mess it had caused.

Abote said that four more hours in my condition, and I would have been dead.

The worst was yet to come. After a terrible bout of vomiting, I was in and out of consciousness, awakened by people taking my vitals and hooking me up to bottles of saline and antibiotics. It crossed my mind that I might be vulnerable to a malaria attack, but I dismissed the possibility: there was so much poison passing through my body that any malaria microbes lying around would never know what hit them.

On Thursday, Abote took out my IV and blessed my departure. I gripped his hand and started to cry. How do you say thanks to the man who has saved your life? Just that, I guess. He responded humbly:

"That's what I am here for, Gary." The next day he would be heading for Great Britain, but he would be handing me over to his associate, Dr. Sebbaale. After warm good-byes from the clinic staff, I headed for Xavier House. Alive.

That first night out of the clinic, I kept thinking that I hadn't so much dodged a bullet in my life—again—as been gently moved out of the bullet's trajectory by that Mystery of love that is beyond all understanding. Each major shift in my life, and each inner awakening, points to God as the author of my existence. I am in God's hands, and I am—and here is the notion that brings me to my knees—*protected*.

Dietrich Bonhoeffer, the German Lutheran theologian who was executed by the Nazis, said that a person's "whole life is an answer to the question and call of God." I am especially aware of this in moments when my life is threatened or my safety jeopardized. Some truths can only be understood from such a vantage point. I believe that God is calling to me amid darkness and pain, vulnerability and uncertainty. And I respond in love.

☼

A week after the surgery, I asked Jim, an American Jesuit working in Kampala, to come to my room and sit with me. I didn't need any words; I told him I just wanted to cry. The pain, trauma, helplessness, and loneliness of the past week had brought me to a breaking point. At that moment, Africa seemed a million light-years away from loved ones. I knew that the anesthesia had plowed into me, disabling those fragile mechanisms that keep me sane and rational. I had been hurled into a depression. The only way over it or through it was to unload with someone I could trust.

I sobbed. From my toes. The hideous past week washed out of me and over me like a rainstorm. It is a stark and empty experience, this business of near death. Jim was a giant of empathy and compassion, saying little, extending his hands—one to which I desperately clung, my other hand holding a handkerchief to my eyes. We prayed at the end. I thought of the line from Proverbs: "Brother helped by brother is a fortress" (18:19).

※

Over the next weeks, I was ferried over to Case Clinic every day, helped by the ever-on-the-spot staff of the JRS Uganda office. My incision was infected, so it had to be swabbed each day with hydrogen peroxide. Not such a lovely experience. I was also inspected by Dr. Sebbaale, a most gracious young man. He'd say to me, "Now, I want you to switch off that part of the brain that says you are sick."

I was walking again, and each night I paced my way around the Jesuit residence, putting in the kilometers. Often there were warm evening rains. They were a wonderful balm for my heart, chasing away the lurking demons of depression and being a comforting companion when I couldn't sleep. As I walked, I prayed over the events of my life and the people who, in God's providence, had been given to me as a gift, beacons of light that bobbed up from the past, surrounding the ocean of my life like a ring of fire. Oddly enough, in all that slow healing from surgery and its inevitable residual pain, I was consoled and thankful. Reinforcing that was the barrage of loving phone calls from local JRS people, solicitous African Jesuits, and friends in the United States.

※

Three weeks after the surgery, Sebbaale put in the final stitches. He asked me, "Do you want me to put you out for fifteen minutes, or just give you a long-needle local?" I told him, "Give me a local, and we can talk." He was dressed in green surgical scrubs, his head covered in a bandanna, his pants tucked into little white boots in which he shuffled about in all those mysterious theaters, working daily miracles. He hovered over my abdomen like a bee above a flower, lacing in the stitches, a master shoemaker sewing up a delicate and beloved old shoe. We gabbed about the day's operations, and I asked him to take me into the head of a surgeon as he faces an emergency appendectomy. He did so, explaining surgical tactics and instincts to me but never taking his eyes off my wound. As he talked, it was so obvious that he loved his work and loved his patients.

How can I explain the extraordinary way in which I was delivered from death? A break, a coincidence, or Providence? Can I dare consider that God acts personally in the direction of my life? Ultimately, I fall back on the fact that there are movements and people and events in my life that I could never have created myself. I just couldn't—my life is a Wild West story.

Then there is the reality of vocation. It seems clear to me that I have been moved right from the conversion to Christianity to being a Jesuit priest, making my hunt in life one of coming to know, love, and serve Christ. God's call—that moment, so hidden and natural—is the first sign of divine care and intervention. If vocation is personal—God's call to me—then why do I run from the possibility that my entire life is personal, that God is moving me, as the Jesuit writer Joseph Tetlow says, *momently*, in every moment?

This is not triumphant self-absorption; it is simply standing before the evidence and truth of my life. If God is involved in my life, then God is involved in my life—period. God's love is palpable, transparent, unyielding, inescapable. I have great affection for the Trappists and Trappistines living and praying off in the boondocks. If they have taught me anything, it is that God can break into a person's life and invite that person to a kind of absurd yes. *Yes, I will follow you; yes, I will live in obscurity; yes, I will live at right angles to the world.*

What about all the people who do not find God acting personally in their lives? I don't know the details of their lives, but insofar as I can accompany them and help them understand the Love that impels and surrounds me, I will. If I have been taken care of, then it is to allow me to bring Love once again into the universe—in this case, Africa—by my touch, by my prayer, by my suffering, by my presence. I am too old now to argue with anyone about the validity of this compelling force in my life and the way I see it. One finally has to take oneself into one's arms and say, *This is who I am, and this is the Love that calls me into existence.*

※

Five weeks after the operation, Dr. Sebbaale took off my last bandage, inspected his work of art, smiled, and said: "Beautiful. Okay, Father, we are finished." Grasping his hand, I told him that he was not only a skilled physician but also a wonderful human being. I asked him to thank the rest of the staff and Dr. Abote. Abote and Sebbaale—what a remarkable pair of human beings and a credit to their profession. They are two of Uganda's great accomplishments.

Later, as I sat in the waiting room, where I had sat so many times in the past five weeks, I almost did not want to leave. I felt like pointing to myself and yelling, "Free at last, free at last!" I resisted the temptation. I walked out of Case Clinic and strolled down Kampala Road, my shoulders back, my head high, surrounded by the organized chaos of a busy city. I was happy, and at peace.

I leaned my face into the wind from the North. Next stop: Adjumani.

Journal: December 2003

The Catechists Welcome Me Home

Today, having returned from Kampala and the Great Appendix Episode, I attended the monthly meeting of the Adjumani catechists in the village of Robidire. As I approached the chapel, the waiting catechists, forty strong, began to rhythmically clap, building to a crescendo as I entered. My body was covered with goose bumps, east to west and north to south. Such warmth. And when they had finished, the lead catechist proclaimed for all in Arabic and then in English, "Rabunna fi kwes; Abuna Gary fi hene. God is good; Father Gary is here." More applause. What a welcome.

Looking out over the catechists in the Robidire chapel, with its deteriorating floors and ancient blackboard and poor lighting, I realized that the church, in its best moments, will be found here. These men and women, refugees all, are the church as it moves and breathes in what might be considered the middle of nowhere. Their faith isn't just a sentiment and is certainly not born of logic; it is rather what gives them life and makes sense of life, and for it they are willing to sacrifice their time and their lives. And I am the number one beneficiary of that sacrifice.

The Kizito

Today I said Mass at the Aliwara chapel, in the southern tip of the Adjumani settlement. It was a small crowd, but that in no way diminished the people's welcome. Everyone greeted me with a smile and a long handshake (if there are ten people in a room or one hundred, one is expected to shake all their hands).

The bonus of the day, maybe even of the month, was the Kizito dancers, twenty-six barefoot balls of energy who decorated the liturgy with their singing and dancing. When they are not dancing, they are responsible for looking after the vulnerable people in the village, particularly the elders. Their name, Kizito, is that of a young nineteenth-century Ugandan martyr. In most of the villages, the Kizito is composed of girls between the ages of five and thirteen. The kids of Aliwara had expressive faces and to-die-for smiles; each wore a homemade blue beret and was dressed in her Sunday "best": a ragged skirt and shirt. They greeted me when I arrived in the village, dancing the car in, and really cranked things up when they led me into the chapel. They proceeded to dance along with all the music of the Mass—and the choir usually has music for every part. Once the music started, an invisible bolt of lightning would pass through them, and in an instant they would be moving in unison: feet, hands, hips, and shoulders.

After Mass, I ducked out into the sunlight, and there they were, waiting for me, along with four curious goats. They gave me a Swahili cheer that involved the clapping of hands and the stomping of feet, and then they sang a welcoming song—for "Abuna Gary"—and danced me over to a chair, which had mysteriously appeared. From there they broke into several formations, singing, stepping, clapping. For thirty minutes I received my own private concert. At different points, one of the little ones would sashay forward and sing a solo, almost in my face, while her sisters hummed and clapped in the background. As I gazed into that beautiful child's face, I thought that my skull would split open from the mystery of it all. These kids: beauty, grace, modesty, dignity. Their words, their music, become flesh and dwell among us.

The wealth of spirit communicated by these children is such a gift. If only others could come and see it and share in it.

The Interview

In Kampala for a break, I had a chance to talk to two Americans, a husband and wife who work with a nonprofit agency in the States that restores old computers and sends them abroad. Ruth has an advanced degree in spirituality from Creighton University and asked to talk with me privately about African spirituality and the African Church. I am no expert on the topic, and I could tell her only what I saw: a communitarian church, a sense of God as absolute, contagious liturgies, and the centrality of the Eucharist. I spoke also about the need to develop an African ecclesiology and how my experience of African spirituality has affected me and my inner life. It comes down to being with the poor and living on the edge; such living renders me more open to love, to compassion, and to another dimension of faith. I find the best in myself here.

Then she asked me about the possibility of death; do I think about it in this volatile world? What could I say? If God, who controls the universe, allows me to be whacked at the Ugandan pass, so be it. After all, God has brought me to this particular place. Do I want to die? No. But I am certainly not here to avoid it. And if it happens, I am trusting in more profound realities than the random killing of the LRA. I have more important things to worry about than the danger of the rebels or of bush life. One takes precautions: like a marathon runner, I know where I am at all times in the race and keep my eyes on the opposition. In the meantime, to use the idea expressed in both Ezekiel and Isaiah, I am heading for the breaches—where the refugees are, where the poor of the world are, where there is vulnerability, and in which someone needs to stand. I do not say that heroically. It is just the way I understand my heart.

Lemi

I returned today to Adjumani after a six-hour drive to the Rhino Camp Refugee Settlement, where I connected with some old friends and conducted business involving three orphan girls in the settlement who I am helping through school. I could not sleep last night, so I wound up walking around the predawn compound, where I ran into Joseph Lemi.

Lemi is the lead elder in the Catholic Church of the Rhino settlement; he oversees the work of elders in the village chapels, listening to and helping them resolve the problems of their people, such as a quarrel over who owns a goat, a conflict between a married couple, a confrontation with local Ugandan nationals, or a dispute with settlement police. In addition, Lemi works closely with the chapel catechists and plays a prominent role in the Sunday Prayers. He is also the night watchman for the JRS compound.

A short man in his fifties, with a broad face and a deep laugh, Lemi is given much respect by the leadership of the villages. When I was director of the project, I helped him out in family matters, with counsel and financial assistance. That morning when I couldn't sleep, we talked and reminisced as the sun, a huge red ball, rose in the east. We laughed about the time that a swarm of grasshoppers passed through the compound and several ended up in my tukul—and underneath my mosquito net. It was one of my first nights in Rhino, and I went into a panic over the insects. Lemi spent the entire night in his sorghum field, flashlight in hand, trying to catch and kill the pesky crop-eaters. He shook his head, remembering that night and commenting that trapping those bugs was like trying to catch the wind.

Though he did not ask for it, I gave him some money; I knew he could use it. He has a large family that includes several children of a deceased brother and sister-in-law. Then he said, "Father, you have done so much for me and my family, and I will always be grateful. You are like a father to my family. I will give my son to you, and we will both be his father. I would send him to you if you want, and he could help you and be with you. You have conceived his life in a different way than me, but by your presence in our lives, surely you have created him and helped to form him. Like a father."

This was Africa talking. There is no greater union here than the union of the family, and beyond that, the clan, and beyond that, the tribe. A person belongs to every one of his blood relations. If a man dies, his children become members of his brother's family.

We stood silently in the growing light of dawn, a bond of intention between us that transcended even blood. I could not take Lemi's son—he knew that—but I could accept his gesture of love and gratitude. It was a moment of splendid intimacy and openness, nothing hidden. I have come so far in distance and years and have experienced so much, but in that moment, I stood before Lemi's expression of love, trembling at its utter newness: "I will give you my son."

When he had departed on his bike for his village, I reflected on another gift of a Son: "God loved the world so much that he gave his only Son" (John 3:16).

LRA Threats

On Friday, the U.S. Embassy in Kampala issued an alert to Americans in northern Uganda that they were possible targets of the LRA. Joseph Kony, the leader of the rebel group, had said in a radio interview that his army would kill U.S. citizens. Those of us in Adjumani were told by the JRS office in Kampala to evacuate west, to a church multipurpose center in Moyo, on the other side of the Nile. It was considered to be a safe zone. We were told to go immediately. So we made our exodus to Moyo, where we joined UNHCR and other NGO staff. Most were not Americans, but they were white; Kony's minions would not discriminate. The first night at the center, I had dinner with people from Germany, Bosnia, Denmark, and South Africa.

I stewed over the situation for a day before I called the JRS director in Kampala and asked for permission to return to Adjumani. I could assure him, based on conversations I'd had with Adjumani district officials, that there was no LRA movement within fifty miles of Adjumani. Privately, I was grappling with another issue. If we are to accompany refugees, then we should stay with them, not cut and run when there is a threat. The director was caught between wanting to support me in my desire to be with the refugees and needing to protect his personnel. It was a corporate decision, a life-and-death decision. But eventually he okayed my return to Adjumani.

That damn Kony. His war has been devastating to northern Uganda. Because of him, resources, land, food, and opportunities to earn income are limited. Because of him, the thousands of Ugandans who have been displaced must search almost daily for water, sanitation facilities, and health care. People are being killed every day, and everyone lives in fear for their lives and for the lives of people they love. Why can't people stop killing and start living?

Wounded in the Bush

After Mass at the village of Esia, the catechist and the congregation and I walked about half a mile into the bush, moving along a ridge that overlooks the Nile. Longa, the catechist, wanted me to anoint a sick man. Like all the other settlement catechists, Longa leads Prayers when I am not there for Mass and assists me when I am there, setting things up, meeting with the choir and dancers, assigning readings, reading the Gospel in Bari, translating for me, and making announcements. I meet with him once a week to practice my Bari pronunciation. He and his wife, Lily, have three children, and they also care for the wife and two children of Longa's deceased brother.

The sick man Longa wanted me to anoint could not come to the chapel because of "mental problems." I had no idea what I would encounter. But I am always coming up against new situations, and I know I just have to take them as they come and use my talents as best I can.

About thirty of us walked in single file on the narrow path, arriving at a small clearing that contained three tukuls arranged around a pile of cooking rocks. Seated on the ground and leaning against a huge rock was Edward. He was clearly suffering; the expression on his face was one of entrenched weariness. He was young, in his early to mid-twenties, and lived with his mother and extended family. He was an epileptic, and one tragic day while his mother was fetching water he had a seizure, fell into the cooking fire, and badly burned one side of his foot.

I was reminded of a street person I knew in Portland, Hansen, who drank himself silly one night and passed out in his skid row hotel room with one foot jammed under a steam radiator. By the next morning, the foot was burned so badly that he wound up having to have it amputated. He was in a wheelchair for the rest of his life.

Edward now has a horrible ulcerated wound. It was covered in some kind of herb that looked like sand, and flies were crawling all over it. It was awful to look at.

I spoke to his mother and made sure that she was clear on the health care Edward needed at the local clinic. She had to be carefully instructed about where the clinic was and when to go. Getting medical care for a loved one is enormously complex and overwhelming for the poor in the bush: health care is limited, money is scarce, and doctors and clinics are often long distances away.

I gave Edward's mother money for medicine for her son, and then we all extended our hands in a final prayer. Everyone present gave Edward a blessing, asking God not only for his healing but for good healers to be brought into his life. I cannot imagine the pain this poor man has gone through. I anointed him and we all prayed the Our Father in Bari: *Baba Likon nye ti kak . . .*

Longa informed me a week later that the family did make it to the clinic and had been transported by UNHCR to a burn facility in Gulu, a large town sixty-five miles southeast of Adjumani. Edward's foot will be saved.

The Wasp from Hell

Yesterday, in the midst of a homily at the Adjumani village of Keyo, I was stung by a wasp (*dara* in Madi). It nailed me on the hand as I was making what I'm sure was a brilliant point. It felt like someone had bitten me. Or shot me. The little rascals build their nests in the teakwood crossbeams that support the grass roof. I guess I interrupted the flight pattern of one of them. I was knocked out of the liturgy for about five minutes, shaking my hand to relieve the pain. All the while, people were bringing me different remedies: kerosene, balm, and fresh mud made from water and the red earth.

Of course, my pained response to the sting was humorous to many people. They looked at me with benevolent pity, as if to say, "You are hurting from the bite of a little dara? You have no idea what hurt is." My hand was swollen, red, and itchy for a week. Word spread quickly through the village chapels: *Get rid of the wasps' nests.* The insects soon became known throughout the settlement as "Abuna Gary's enemy."

The Persistent Widow

Early in my pastoral work with the refugees, I determined that the best way to break open the Gospel was through drama: the people acting out the stories themselves. Yesterday, at Umwia chapel, the Gospel was Jesus' parable of the unscrupulous judge and the persistent widow who demands justice against those who have done her wrong (Luke 18:1–8).

I chose a no-nonsense woman, Almaria, to be the widow, and a highly respected elder, Luka, to play the role of the powerful judge. They leaped into the drama, Almaria first complaining about a neighbor's goats wandering through her property and eating her maize. At first, the judge told her he couldn't be bothered, and all the people in the chapel jeered at him; the second time she came to him with her complaint, he gave her more time to make her case but in the end referred to her as just another whining woman who was probably exaggerating the whole thing. This of course agitated the women in the chapel, who knew well what it feels like to be disregarded and belittled. There was more jeering from the audience and a defiant promise by Almaria that she would be back. The third time, she knocked once on the judge's door and then sat down and refused to move. Judge Luka was exasperated and capitulated to widow Almaria's demands. The people in the chapel applauded.

Afterward, I asked Luka and Almaria why they did what they did. When they gave their answers, I turned to the people and asked their opinion. And then I posed a question to all: Why did Jesus tell this parable? A young teenager led the way with "God created us out of love and will answer our calls with that love. And God expects his creatures to deal with each other with love and to do it fairly." Everyone proudly nodded at such wisdom from one of Umwia's younger sons.

Whenever I see the catechist from Umwia, Aswan, we both laugh about the persistent widow's coup de grâce: sitting at the judge's door, an immovable object not to be denied.

A Noise in the Night

Every night around eleven o'clock, after four hours of more or less continual operation, the power goes out in Adjumani and the night becomes black, dotted with a kerosene lamp here and there and maybe a rare solar-powered lamp. Late June nights are warm from the day's abundant sun and frequent rains.

At a late hour on one of those nights, a dozen armed members of the Lord's Resistance Army entered Adjumani from the surrounding tall grass and trees of the bush and moved silently through the eastern part of town toward Holy Redeemer Orphanage, directed by the Sisters of the Sacred Heart.

The LRA operates in the north and east of Uganda and specializes in the slaughter of innocent people: a village is looted and burned to the ground, its inhabitants locked in their flaming houses; a bus is shot up on the way south to Kampala, its passengers pulled out and hacked to death; a health clinic is raided and robbed, its workers murdered; a pickup truck is ambushed, its passengers butchered and the truck torched; grade schools, high schools, and seminaries are attacked, and ten, twenty, thirty students abducted.

Abduction of children is the most depressing and horrifying tactic of the LRA. In the last seventeen years, the number has approached twenty thousand. These child "recruits" are forced into submission and made to carry weapons; almost immediately after they have been abducted, they are terrorized into committing their own atrocities. These can involve beating to death one of their classmates (or be bludgeoned to death themselves) or plundering their own village and killing their relatives so that they will have no place to return to. The girls are given to LRA commanders as sex slaves. Many who escape their abductors come back with unwanted children and a host of sexually transmitted diseases. As the months pass, the abducted lose track of their personal lives, their family culture, and any kind of moral code. They learn indifference and brutality. Children are transformed into killers. Some escape. Some are rescued. Some are killed.

The dozen LRA soldiers, between sixteen and twenty-five years old, stopped at the parish in Adjumani that night in June and awakened Father Zachary, a member of the Apostles of Jesus. Zachary was roughed up, his room ransacked, and most of his personal belongings taken. He was then forced at gunpoint to proceed with the LRA people to the orphanage, two hundred meters from the church. Once the security of the orphanage—a flimsy wooden gate with a terrified gatekeeper—was breached, they advanced to the dormitory of the orphans. One of the Sacred Heart sisters sleeping in a residence adjacent to the dormitory awoke, realized what was happening, and pleaded with the abductors to stop. They forced her back into her room, gathered the now frightened and screaming children, ages seven to eighteen, nine of them girls, and began to run them single file out of the compound. Two other sisters awoke at the noise, but it was too late. It was about two in the morning. One of the sisters called the local contingent of the Ugandan army, placed there by the government for the town's protection. They arrived hours later.

Because of the LRA, a great swath of northern Uganda writhes in social convulsion. It is a region sabotaged by uncertainty and tragedy. There are more than 1.5 million internally displaced people in the North—in a country of 28 million—living in squalid government protection camps. Malnutrition, cholera, tuberculosis, measles, dysentery, and malaria plow through these camps. Here are the real death statistics of this war, the unseen bottom of the killing iceberg. And to make things worse, the camps are easy targets of attacks by LRA soldiers, who circle their victims—indigenous Ugandans—like sharks. And with all this chaos comes a pervading sense of helplessness and hopelessness. Recently, Johan Van Hecke, a Belgian member of the European Parliament who has long experience in African humanitarian causes, especially in Uganda, said, "This ongoing war is the worst abuse of human rights in the world, and the West has forgotten it."

Local religious leaders and civil leaders have tried to broker peace deals, but their efforts have failed; so the slaughter continues daily. In all the years I have been in this country, I cannot recall a day when the Ugandan press did not report an LRA incident. In spite of its talk of making advances against the insurgency, the Ugandan government appears impotent, and the Ugandan military often outmaneuvered. The army does manage to kill many members of the LRA, if one can believe the reports. They kill the kids who kill. Kids who were once students, seminarians, and joyful young boys and girls.

☀

In the pitch-dark night, Father Zachary brought up the rear of the line of children, and at an opportune time, heart pounding, he slipped off into the tall grass of the bush. The LRA and their latest victims moved east, grabbing a few adults along the way, who, if normal procedure was followed, were then killed in the bush by the abducted children. One kills or is killed. It is the kind of chilling pressure that most fourteen-year-olds will cave in to. Zachary waited until the sounds faded away and cautiously made his way back to the church. Several of the children later escaped and returned, but some have not been seen or heard of since.

Although JRS works primarily with the refugees from Sudan who live in northern Uganda, the LRA affects our work and inflicts its terror directly and indirectly on the refugees. Father Zachary is part of the JRS pastoral team in Adjumani, and the Sisters of the Sacred Heart have deep connections with all of us who work in the North. The Holy Redeemer Orphanage is adjacent to the living compound of JRS International staff. For us, a noise in the night is no longer just a noise in the night. Here in Adjumani two years ago, a bus was ambushed several miles out of town, and many of the JRS staff lost relatives and friends. A year ago, the LRA rampaged through refugee villages in a southern zone of our pastoral commitment area. Sudanese were killed, children abducted. Recently, after dropping off a JRS project director at an airfield near Labone, Sudan, a driver was stopped by the LRA and murdered along with his two teenage passengers, and the car was burned. The Sudanese driver, a father of two, was twenty-six. A few weeks ago, the LRA hit a health clinic eight miles from Adjumani, stole all its drugs and kidnapped the workers. A week later, two secondary school girls from Nimule, a Sudanese town on the border of Uganda, were abducted as they crossed into Uganda to pay a visit to friends.

On top of all this, the JRS projects in Southern Sudan and northern Uganda must frequently suspend pastoral and education work in targeted areas because of the security risk. Chapels cannot be visited, and schools are closed. There is a lurking anxiety throughout the North and the East. Where and when will they hit again? Are we seeing a slow version of Rwanda, not tribe against tribe with a million deaths a month, but crazed warriors against their own, innocent, people? Another ten years, another twenty thousand dead? Another thirty thousand children abducted?

Father Zachary is a soft-spoken and unobtrusive man, a native of the north of Uganda. His upper lip quivers as he quietly recalls the night he was captured. His ordeal was small, he points out, compared to what happened to the children who were abducted. Had he not escaped, he knows, he would have been killed—too much extra luggage to carry. A man without guile, Zachary makes no big deal about his life of sacrifice, puts on no airs, and gently goes about his pastoral work in the Adjumani refugee villages. He admits to being shaken by that night, but he is determined to go on and serve.

Standing back and looking at this attack on the orphanage and the years of Uganda's torture by carnage, one must admire Father Zachary's commitment to his ministry. He inspires me; he is the human antidote to the poison. On the edges and within the ebb and flow of these events stands the Jesuit Refugee Service, walking with him. As JRS serves the refugees of the twenty-year civil war in Sudan, it always, warily and wearily, has to watch the LRA. JRS, too, is an antidote. By its work, it counteracts—with many others—the poison of the LRA's rejection of each human's dignity. It seeks, like Zachary, to carry on the mission of Christ, to accompany all those rendered homeless by the raiders of the night. It serves the refugee and the displaced and all who are hurled into chaos by the likes of the LRA. It advocates for the afflicted, saying to the world that the madness must stop, and that as long as brothers and sisters are wounded, the whole world is wounded.

Yayo

At first, I saw only her right hand. I was inside her tukul, and a hand appeared on the dirt floor at the opening of the hut. Her left hand appeared soon after, then her head, then her emaciated body. She was a Madi woman named Andalinda Yayo, the mother of the woman cate-chist of the village of Magburu. Her daughter had accompanied me to Yayo's tukul because she wanted the sacrament of reconciliation. Yayo inched in, having crawled from a nearby latrine. Once inside the nine-by-nine-foot room, she groped her way to an empty grain sack stretched out on the floor, which she probably used as a bed. She was crippled with what looked like arthritic knees and had a tumor on her left leg between the knee and the thigh. She was around sixty years old but looked to be over a hundred. And she was blind.

She was so happy that I was there that you would have thought Jesus himself had dropped by. Her daughter introduced us. When I pro-nounced her name, she gazed up at me as if she could see; there was so much in those sightless eyes. Here was the feminine face of God, again. With her daughter's help, she had me practice saying her name. "Ya-YO," she stressed, placing the accent on the second syllable. "Ya-YO." I duti-fully pronounced her name until I got it right, whereupon she sat back more comfortably on her mat and smiled approvingly.

Her daughter left, and Yayo made her confession in Madi. There was no translator present, so I did not understand what she was say-ing. In this kind of situation when I don't speak the language, I simply listen earnestly, occasionally picking up a word, but for the most part accepting that what is important is the penitent's intention. Of course, it is frustrating not knowing the various languages of the settlement, because language can take me to the heart of a person, and, from the penitent's point of view, a word of counsel or affirmation can console and inspire. I must depend on what I see in the penitent's face, and on the Holy Spirit to make up the difference. And although I cannot speak the language, I can still make a personal connection. Many come to me to make their confessions because they trust me and my love.

At what seemed like the conclusion of Yayo's confession, I asked her in Arabic if she was finished. She nodded, then reached out and grabbed my hands. I prayed in English, and then prayed the absolution in Arabic. Yayo's face was turned up at mine, and she gave me an irrepressible toothless smile. At that point, she sank into a totally absorbed prayer of thanksgiving.

Where are the mystics of this world? Are they sitting on crummy grain sacks on dirt floors in northern Uganda? Are they among the blind and the crippled? I'd put my money on Yayo. She seems to live in a state of what St. Ignatius would call consolation without cause. In other words, she is always in the presence of the heart of God. As I left her tukul, I whispered into her ear the Arabic words *As-salaamu alaikum, akhawaat, salaam* ("Peace be with you, my sister, peace"). Her face was like sunrise on the Nile valley.

There were other confessions that day, many of women, young and old, wearing rags and nothing on their feet, their straight proud necks carrying chiseled and lean faces, their bodies smelling of sweat and unyielding work in the fields or in the home. What is it about these women that so gets to me? Their simplicity? Their directness? I think I am touching a grace that cuts through the hard rocks of the refugee's life, something deeper, something that strengthens them through whatever suffering life throws at them. It is faith, their unshakable faith. Nothing obstructs their sense and love of God: not hardship, not death of loved ones, not drought, not war, not the empty stomachs of their children.

At the end of each confession, I would pray in English, and the woman would watch my face as I had watched hers. I would pray that God would fill her heart with the knowledge of God's love for her. Then I would give her absolution in her own tongue (Bari, Madi, Acholi, or Arabic), which I had memorized over time, and reach over and grasp her hand and say in Arabic, as I had to Yayo, "Peace, my sister, peace."

I have known and wept with and consoled the Sudanese refugee woman, particularly as she is a mother. When you know her as a mother, you understand how she can age so quickly. The Sudanese refugee mother is poor and frequently has a baby strapped to her back or nursing at her breast. She is always working—sweeping, cooking, cleaning, carrying huge loads on her head—and is often pregnant; most likely, she has had children who have died of malaria. She is friendly and long-suffering, loves to talk and joke with her sisters, is close to her tribe and clan, most often cannot read or write, and is born into and suffers from a rigid male-dominated culture. She dies young. Often she is old before her time, but she possesses an interior beauty that endures until she dies. She would die in an eye blink for her family. I have buried her after childbirth. I have anointed her as she was dying of some tropical disease. I have given her alms when she has extended her hand, fingers lost to leprosy. I have raced my car over impossible roads to get her to a clinic where she can deliver her baby. I have been with her when she is dying of the shock of a breech birth, a little foot sticking out of her body. I have helped her younger daughters continue with their studies in the face of a cultural attitude that educating a girl child is not necessary—an attitude she has faced firsthand. I have fallen in love with the African mother, whose goodness and beauty have left me shaking.

One day, such a mother, Mary Kenyi, came to me. Her old body was covered in a threadbare dress. She often came by, asking for a few beans or some grain and sometimes for a blanket. She has nothing, not even a son or daughter to care for her in her old age. All of her children were killed in the Sudan civil war, along with her husband. I saw her, a long walking stick in hand, coming toward me as I was conversing with a staff member outside our compound. I thought to myself, perhaps with an edge of irritation, *I wonder what she will be asking for today?* She carried a small plastic bag and handed it to me, giving me a smile that would capture the heart of the most heartless.

In the bag was a gift for me.

Three eggs.

The Beautiful Mouth of Jacelin Ojok

A friend was lamenting to me the fact that she could not do more to alleviate the suffering of the world's people. Had she taken the wrong path in life? Could she have been more of an activist? I responded to her in a letter:

> We do what we can do, as you have. We move and choose according to our lights and discernment. Sometimes this involves the heroic. And yet, it is true that although most of us would like to be the spark of love that sets the world on fire, life rarely offers such a scenario. We do our thing minute by minute, day by day, year by year. Sanctity, it seems to me, occurs in this fashion.
>
> When you reach out to the vulnerable, it helps: pain is embraced and sometimes removed. That is a good and, I think, holy response to what moves in you. To me, such an outreach of the heart is a sign of Christ's heart moving in the world, moving in his Body. When we can do nothing but watch and mourn, it is Christ's heart that watches and mourns. When we are compassionate or when we tell the truth or when we express anger over injustice, can we not say it is an incarnation in our own lives of the heart of Christ? And when we intervene in

the darkness and chaos of the universe, isn't it Christ's action? Isn't it his love?

Like Jesus with the blind man of Jericho, or the men who brought their crippled companion for healing and had to hack through a roof in order to lower the stretcher down in front of Jesus, we can make things happen as we are driven by the least of our brothers and sisters. Sometimes we can only love at a distance. How we are led in different ways and on different paths is purely an act of the freedom of God, the gift of God's grace. We are witnesses to a mystery of human care and compassion that is beyond us and yet benevolently inhabits us, like the heart of the lover inhabits her beloved.

The following is a story of one way in which these observations were lived out.

☀

I was at Arra, about ten miles north of Adjumani, for Mass. The village lies along the Nile, but it receives little rain. The ground is dry, and the maize and sorghum do not grow with energy and abundance, as they do in other places.

It was my first time in Arra, a village composed primarily of poor Madi tribe members from the eastern part of Southern Sudan. Madra, a catechist in his early thirties, greeted me and led me to the tree that served as the temporary chapel for the congregation. The forty or so people there were cheerful and curious.

While listening to Madra read the Gospel, I saw, moving along the outskirts of the congregation, a young girl, maybe ten years of age, shabbily dressed, bearing a child on her back. The child was probably her sibling, I thought, since eldest daughters often pack a younger sister or brother who is not walking. At one point, our eyes met. Hers were sad, accentuated in her round face.

There was something else. She had a cleft lip.

She was on my mind throughout the prayers. After Mass, I inquired about her. Her name was Jacelin Ojok. I asked to see her and her parents. It turned out that she had no father, and her mother did not live in Arra but near the Sudan border; for whatever reason, she could not attend to her daughter, so she sent Jacelin to live with her aunt and her uncle, who was the catechist, Madra.

Madra brought Jacelin to me. The baby on her back was her cousin, and Jacelin handed her over to her aunt, Lilly. Jacelin was dressed in a torn T-shirt and a drab skirt that almost touched her bare feet. I put my arm over her shoulder. She was fearful and never took her eyes off the ground as I spoke with her uncle and aunt. It was like a sadistic surgeon had cut a wedge in her upper lip, right up to the nose, exposing her teeth so that she would be doomed always to have a crooked smile. A cleft lip is one manifestation of nature at its blind and brutal worst. It is a heartbreaking disfigurement. I explained to Madra and the other concerned elders who were around that a team of plastic surgeons in Kampala who specialized in repairing cleft lips came periodically to local northern hospitals. They did their work free of charge. Would Madra and Lilly be interested in arranging for the doctors to see Jacelin? They would.

I turned to Jacelin. She was shy, clearly self-conscious as she talked with me, monosyllabically, through a translator. She occasionally glanced up at me as if she had been warned not to look too long. It was probably the first time she had ever talked to a white person, so she was apprehensive. All this attention was too much, and she began to cry. I asked her through Madra if she would like to have her lip fixed. She uttered an "Ahhh," the Madi expression for yes.

This condition is not rare in the bush; there are many children so afflicted, but often they are hidden away. A cleft lip can be a result of many things, one of which is the poor condition of the mother during pregnancy, because of malnutrition, disease, or the ingestion of bad food or medicine.

There are obstacles to repairing cleft lips in the bush. Often parents don't understand the condition and that it can be surgically corrected, and of course there is the cost of such a procedure: many parents, confronted with any kind of disease or disability in their child, often do nothing about it, because they think they cannot afford it. And there are those who think that a cleft lip is a function of God's will, a divine punishment. Why try to change it? And, too, female children especially are denied medical care; it is a sad fact of the culture that females are often considered expendable.

Where does God stand on all this, on this disability, on the disabilities of the world, on the cripples I see crawling down the main streets of Adjumani, or the emaciated people begging in downtown Kampala, or the children dying of malaria in Moyo, or the lepers of Arua? Why does this happen? Is God uncaring? And where do I stand?

I think of my friend and former college roommate, Wells, who died inch by inch in his bed from multiple sclerosis. Seeing him trapped in a useless body and feeling helpless to do anything about it used to hurl me into a crisis of faith. I have read the book of Job. The explanation for Job's undeserved misery is supposed to be found in the last chapters of the book, where God answers his cries. I've never found the answers satisfactory. The fact is that no one has ever provided a satisfactory answer to why people kill without cause, or why children are made to suffer, or why people are knocked down by disability, starvation, oppression, or seemingly endless grief.

I looked at Jacelin, and I was confused yet again. Such innocence, such unfair suffering. But in such moments, one act helps me rise out of my confusion; one act makes sense in the surrounding storm: holding Jacelin and the Jacelins of this world in my arms. At that moment, my engines of compassion were ignited. I was determined to bring beauty to her life. Maybe part of the answer to why these things happen is that we are called by God to carry our broken and battered brothers and sisters on our backs. And in doing so, we discover that they carry us and facilitate the birth of wisdom and love in us that never would have occurred had we not encountered their suffering. Wells used to say, "You need me in your life, Gar, you need me." Part of the answer to the mystery of broken creation is in my unbroken creative arms.

Two months after I met Jacelin, I was back in Arra to check on the repairs to the chapel. I was accompanied by Father Idro, an African priest with whom I work in the refugee settlements. On our way out of the village, we stopped by Jacelin's family compound. Madra was not there, so Idro and I talked with Jacelin's aunt, Lilly. Jacelin stood nearby, her cousin on her back. She remembered me, but still she was afraid. I suppose it was confusing to her: why would I be interested in her? She watched silently as we talked. She knew we were talking about her.

We discussed the plastic surgery, and Lilly was concerned about how she would take care of Jacelin at the hospital. In Ugandan hospitals, food is not provided, so the patient's family has to make provisions for that. I told her not to worry: I would make the necessary arrangements. It is such a terrible in-your-face truth that in much of Africa, people cannot afford medical help or all the logistical necessities. And even when medical care is free, there is always the problem of the impossible distances from a bush village to a town hospital. In the bush, you can't just get on the phone and call your local doctor, or jump on a bus and head for the emergency room.

As Idro and I were about to leave the compound, I decided to take Jacelin's photo. She wanted to put on a better dress, the replacement another used-up and faded beauty. God, it broke my heart to see her effort to appear nice. I took her photo, asking Idro to tell her in Madi to smile. She gave a twisted smile, but a trusting one. We said good-bye.

I thought to myself as we pulled out of the village, *What is she making of all this?* She had won my heart, hands down. Jacelin was special; her becoming whole had become my magnificent obsession.

※

A month and a half later, I was back in Arra for Mass. I was looking for Jacelin, and behold, as I started the Mass I saw her sitting in the back, her ever-present cousin strapped to her back. Clearly, they were buddies. We caught each other's eye, and she smiled her wonderful smile. After Mass, I asked to see her and her uncle and aunt, and while I talked with Madra and Lilly, Jacelin stood beside me, her hand in mine. I asked her at the conclusion of our talk if she understood that we were talking about the proposed operation on her lip. She nodded. Did she still want to do it? Yes.

O God, I prayed, *let this operation happen.*

※

The plastic surgeons were due to arrive in the North in two months. On a whim, I called the hospital, inquiring about registration for Jacelin, and was told that the surgical team would be arriving in *two days*. I had to organize everything quickly, in the midst of a packed schedule. The

Providence of the situation scared me. What on earth prompted me to call today?

Four days later, I picked up Jacelin. She had everything she possessed with her: the pitifully shabby clothes on her back. Her aunt, Lilly, gathered her few things, mostly for her nursing daughter, Margaret, and we all piled into the pickup. Everyone was quiet and expressionless.

When we arrived at Adjumani hospital, the person in charge met us and guided us to an intake room where other children were gathering. I asked how many would be coming for surgery. Possibly sixty, he said, but it would most likely be in the neighborhood of forty. Already that morning, some surgeries were being performed, on kids who had come from Moyo, across the Nile, the night before. There were three doctors, all African surgeons from Kampala.

As the intake room started to fill up, the astonishing truth of the extent of the deformity in this region fell on me like a falcon. I became fearful, repelled as I always am around tropical diseases and disfigurements. But I am here because I believe I was called to this place and, more important, to be present to the people God brings into my life. It was obvious that only Jacelin could teach me a new level of compassion and how to receive a new kind of love. My heart is bigger than my petty descents into revulsion. A person's behavior or appearance does not tell me who I am, or inhibit what I am called to be. I looked over at Jacelin. Her eyes got bigger by the second, and I realized that for the first time in her life she could see that there were people like her. Her little eyes darted back and forth as now one child, then another came in, usually accompanied by an adult, bearing the same birth wound that had plagued her for ten years.

Her heart was moving at right angles to mine: she had no fear. Suddenly, she was not alone, no longer an alien in the universe; she was surrounded by fellow travelers, shy and wounded like she was. They, in turn, were staring at her, equally and happily dumfounded. A small boy walked past me and gave me the smile of the day. I stepped outside. I am not sure Jacelin would have understood my tears. Being in that room was utterly overwhelming. It was like visiting another planet, a planet where all the inhabitants bear the mark of a terrible war, and in the midst of the rubble one of the residents welcomed me as if nothing was wrong. Maybe nothing was.

I left for the JRS office an hour later, promising to return in the late afternoon with items Jacelin and her aunt and cousin would need for the night: a sleeping mat, two blankets, and food money. When I returned, Jacelin and Lilly were in a holding room waiting for a ward assignment. Sitting next to Jacelin was the same little boy who had knocked me out with his smile. There, among all the other patients and parents flying back and forth, after years of discomfort and isolation, these two young human beings had formed a conspiracy of camaraderie. Tomorrow they would go in for surgery.

☀

The next day, Ratib and I went by the hospital. Jacelin had come out of surgery about an hour before. She and Lilly were in a ward full of anxious family members and children who were in recovery. The room was noisy and full of smells. There were no lights in the hospital, so the room was lit indirectly by the late afternoon sun. I caused a mild sensation when I came in, the white man attending to someone he knew. Since Jacelin was still under anesthesia, all I could do was talk briefly to her aunt, with Ratib translating. Jacelin was lying on her side, her face turned away. I peered over her shoulder and looked at her new mouth. It was beautiful, complete.

Does a father feel like this when he holds his new child for the first time? I put my hand on her head and whispered a prayer of gratitude for all the children in that ward of miracles.

I asked Lilly if she needed anything, and she requested a mosquito net for Jacelin. The mosquitoes were thick in the hospital. As Ratib and I were driving back to the JRS office, I thought of another friend, Robert, who had died in his early thirties of AIDS. He left a note for me to read after his death: "If all goes well, I'll be watching over you," it said.

Pray for her, Robert. Watch over my little friend.

☀

In hospitals in the United States, the smell is always antiseptic, of Clorox, freshly washed sheets, and scrubbed-down floors and windows. There was none of that in Adjumani hospital: it smelled of ablutions and food and a busy hive of people socializing.

Jacelin, now up and about, was her serious little self, but she was looking at me more, trusting me. After a number of delays—dealing with medicine and final check-offs and the official release—we were able to take her home. We would pick her up in a week for the removal of the stitches and a final checkup.

From the day I saw Jacelin circling the crowd at that first Mass in Arra, it had been my mission to help her become whole. Now the deed was done. I wanted to take that little girl in my arms and hold her and hold her and hold her. There is a steely resolve in refugee children; they accept hardship and deprivation as part of daily life. They learn the truth early: life is not fair.

☀

A week later, Ratib picked up Jacelin and Lilly at their compound and brought them to Adjumani for the removal of the stitches. Afterward, he came by the JRS office to announce that the stitches were out. Following him was a barefoot Jacelin. Holding her hand, I took her around the facility and introduced her to the JRS staff. I felt like a proud father showing off his beloved child. The staff had been following Jacelin's story for months, and now here she was in front of them.

At the end of our visit, when it was time for them to return home, Jacelin and Lilly climbed into the pickup, bound for Arra, the quest for her happiness and wholeness completed. JRS had been raided: my heart had been taken prisoner.

That night, as I was explaining the entire experience to a visitor, I started to cry. I don't remember at what part in the story I broke down, but this can be said: in the moments of telling the story of Jacelin Ojok, I was engaging the most generous part of my heart and the mysterious experience of my capacity to love. I felt so bound to that little girl.

> So all of us, in union with Christ, form one body, and as
> parts of it we belong to each other. (Romans 12:5)

My life is rooted in and driven by this certainty. In all the successes and failures, ups and downs, crazy and sane moments of my life, I have learned that I become who I am through my relationships with other human beings. And in those relationships, I uncover the tracks of God's relationship with me. Jacelin was a dramatic illustration of this. I discovered myself in my love for her and her love for me—as unarticulated as it was. Together, we discovered the love of God.

Journal: June 2004

Murder in Dubaju

Two catechists, Calisto and Juma, and I conducted a seminar at Dubaju yesterday. It is Calisto's village and the seminar was held in his chapel. While we were waiting for people to arrive, we received word that a six-year-old girl had been killed during the night. The news was shocking in itself, but she had been killed, her neck broken, by her own father. He had come home drunk. His wife was staying overnight at a cousin's home in order to help with the harvesting of roof grass early the next morning. An older son, eight years old, was asleep during the whole episode.

The people buzzed about the tragedy during the seminar breaks. Later in the day, the village chairman came to me and asked if I would transport the father to the police station in nearby Ciforo, Uganda, accompanied by village security. I said I would. It was really the responsibility of the police to transport the man, but they were not around. Since it looked as if this guy had murdered his own daughter, I wanted to be of assistance.

Eventually, the village elders brought the man to the chapel, where Ratib had parked the pickup; he looked disheveled and shocked and afraid. He was tied with a rope around his waist, walking ahead of the man holding the rope and another man who was carrying a long-bladed cutting tool called a panga. The man might as well have been a goat being driven ahead of his master. He was directed to the pickup, and

Ratib, concerned that he might try to escape or kill himself, had the Dubajo men tie him securely to the bed of the truck.

What could have brought this man to kill his own daughter? The little girls here are so beautiful and bright and effusive. They snare my heart regularly. As we traveled to the police station, Ratib, the father of two young girls, tried to grasp the incomprehensible tragedy of it all. He kept saying over and over, occasionally with a hitch in his voice, "It's unbelievable, Father, it's unbelievable."

We dropped the man off at the police station; he was broken and will live under the curse of his own stupidity for the rest of his life. He'll forever be looking over his shoulder as revenging relatives seek retribution.

As we drove Calisto and Juma back to Dubajo, I made sure that Calisto understood that he would have to be an agent of healing in his community. He knew this, of course, being charged with the pastoral responsibilities in his village, but I saw my role as priest as one of guiding and affirming him. I also wanted to ensure that he would communicate to the mother of the dead child the willingness of JRS to help with any short-term needs. It was a vivid moment of accompanying the refugees. The next day, a field officer with the UNHCR dropped by the JRS office with the local police to get my perspective on what had happened.

The Whole World Is Watching

Ah, the sacred and the secular, the ridiculous and the sublime. I am reminded of their intersection all the time.

Recently, catechists Osura and Kenyi and I were leading a seminar on the sacraments in Cochi, a village in the Palorinya settlement. During a break, I asked where I could find a latrine. I was led to a circular enclosure made of papyrus, about five feet high. On the ground inside the circle were a bunch of flat rocks. The latrine appeared to be located in the dead center of the village. People started coming out of their tukuls to greet me and stare—a white man walking through a village is a sight to behold.

As I stood in the circle, visible from the neck up, all the kids in the village who had gathered to look at me stood there and watched. I tried to act nonchalantly. But all those curious little eyes gave me performance anxiety. Of course, I can't blame them—this was probably the first time they had ever seen a *cawaja* relieve himself in their village, maybe even the first time in all of Cochi history that a white man had set foot in the latrine. As the children gawked and giggled at uncomfortable me, all I could think of was the refrain of the protestors being beaten by police at the 1968 Democratic National Convention in Chicago: "The whole world is watching, the whole world is watching."

Nyumanzi Chapel

About two years ago, we had to pull out of ministry to Nyumanzi because of LRA jabs into the area of Adjumani through which we had to travel to get to the village. Recently, we decided that it was okay to return, on the counsel of local government officials. The LRA has been on the run lately and is now located, for the most part, in Southern Sudan.

Driving out with Ratib, I was depressed and spooked by the evidence of self-evacuation: empty and burned-out tukuls, uncultivated land, virtually no people. That we are now into the third month of the dry season only accentuated the forlorn, desperate quality of the land. Oh, if these trees could talk, what grief had they witnessed?

Of course, the thought went through my mind that those LRA fools might suddenly pop out into the middle of the road, shooting away. The grass on either side of the road was very high, a perfect hiding place. As we turned each new corner, I couldn't help but think, *What a great place for an ambush.* What a bunch of jackals those LRA soldiers are, keeping the people in a state of fear, cornering and culling the vulnerable, fulfilling their bloodlust.

In the end, everything turned out happily. Imperio Modi, a bold and zealous catechist, only recently back from two years of training and the head catechist for his village of Ibibiaworo, has resurrected the Nyumanzi chapel. He oversees the work of three other catechists in the chapels of three nearby villages. A Bari-speaking Kuku by tribe, Modi is fluent in Arabic and English, an excellent teacher, and an enthusiastic leader of Prayers. His wife has been sick ever since I met her, two years ago, suffering from a variety of tropical diseases. They have five children.

We had Mass for the first time in years in the rehabilitated chapel. Seven adults and about twenty children were present. The people were happy. So was I.

Lodu

One of the smart young catechists in the Palorinya Refugee Settlement, Virgilio Lodu, recently returned from a school to which I had sent him to learn theology and techniques for teaching it. He returned in time to help us with a seminar in the village of Kali.

Lodu is a Kuku by tribe and speaks Bari as his mother tongue, but his English is excellent and he is conversant with several other languages. He is the catechist for the Palorinya settlement village of Orinya, a man very solicitous for his people and aware of their problems. He has a young wife and three children. He came to Uganda in the nineties from an area in the far southeast of Sudan. What I appreciate most about him is not just his quick mind and sound grasp of theology, but also his easy smile and deep chuckling laugh.

At the seminar, Lodu was a bit nervous, but he understood the material well, had the respect of the people, and could speak all the languages of the people present. About half an hour into the give-and-take in a lesson on Christian community, he received his baptism of fire in the form of an intoxicated woman who sauntered in and announced her arrival from the back of the chapel, bellowing out in Bari: "Y Karin ti Monye, ko ti Tore, ko Mulokutyo Loke"—"In the name of the Father, and the Son, and the Holy Spirit." All eyes turned from Lodu to the woman, who made her wobbly way up to the front of the chapel. Reaching the altar, she fell to her knees on the dirt floor and began to utter her prayers—loudly. Lodu was distracted by the abruptness of the interruption; his presentation was in danger of being decapitated. I was sitting off to the side, looking directly at the woman. Out of the corner of her eye, in the midst of her sensational disruption, she spotted me. She nodded to me and said in Bari, "You are most welcome, Father." Then she went back to her loud and ostentatious prayers.

Eventually she was removed, going defiantly limp like a sack of sweet potatoes and condemning the infidels—three very displeased chapel women—who were dragging her out. I suggested we take a break so that the problem could be sorted out and Lodu could regain his composure. When we reconvened, Lodu aced his presentation and received a heart-warming ovation. We had a good laugh about the woman in our review of the day.

The Disabled at Lereje Chapel

I was in the Palorinya Refugee Settlement again this morning, in the village of Lereje. It is located at the end of an enchanting drive, on a road that parallels the Nile and moves alternately through swamps and groves of coconut trees.

I was conducting a seminar for the first time in the village, so the people were curious, having never seen me before. The village has only recently been created by the UNHCR, for refugees fleeing LRA activities in Southern Sudan. Joseph Kony, the leader of the LRA, under enormous pressure from the Ugandan army, has moved much of his operation into Southern Sudan, which means that outlying villages in the region are being attacked and major roads are being interdicted by Kony's people. Frightened for their lives, the Sudanese from the area have fled to transition camps in northern Uganda, most of them in the Palorinya Refugee Settlement. A small chapel has been established in Lereje, a tree under which religious services and seminars are held.

Osura and Lodu, two of the catechists, did presentations on church leadership and the use of talents and gifts in the local church. There was intense participation. What I will always remember about the day, besides the great work of Osura and Lodu, is the number of handicapped people who came to the seminar. I talked to a fifteen-year-old girl, Keji, who had been blind since she was five. Her father was also blind. Had she ever had any schooling? No. Did she want an education? Yes, but how? I told her of a school for the blind in Moyo and asked if she would like the staff to come out to see her. Yes, yes, yes! There was another blind person, a man who had lost his sight while serving in the SPLA. It happened in Juba, Sudan, but not in combat; a comrade who was cleaning his loaded rifle next to him accidentally pulled the trigger. In an instant, the man lost vision in both eyes. They were surgically removed, so he is left with empty eye sockets.

Then, during a break in the presentations, I saw a crippled man coming around the pump of a nearby well. He walked on his hands, on which he wore flip-flops, and swung his stick legs through his arms. He made his way right up to me, removed one of the thongs from his hand, reached up, and shook my hand, saying in perfect English, "My name is Joseph, Father Gary. You are most welcome to our village." Therewith we began a good and long friendship. Whenever I was in the region of Lereje, I always made a point to visit with Joseph.

It is the same old story, but always new: in the presence of the poor I find myself.

Of Malaria and Munu Quicksand

Munu is in the jungle of the Palorinya Refugee Settlement, perhaps ten minutes off the main road to Yumbe, a major town near the Sudan border. The Munu chapel is humble, about eight rows of log benches under a gigantic lulu tree.

Five of us—catechists Wurube, Dima, Marine, and Jame and I—were in the village to conduct a seminar, but the chapel's charismatic catechist, Christopher Munele, was very ill with malaria, so the seminar had been canceled, unbeknownst to us. We decided to drive to Munele's compound, greet him, pray with him, and anoint him. The rains had started the day before, so the path to his compound was soggy, but passable. When we arrived, he came out to greet us. It was shocking to see him. The poor guy, always an Ichabod Crane of a man, looked as if he had just been released from an oppressive prison that never fed him. His hair was the ginger color that indicates malnutrition. He walked toward us with the help of a cane. Having seen this disease wreak its havoc on hundreds over the years, I thought what he had was beyond malaria, a kind of super-malaria, whacking him from one end to the other, inside and out.

At six feet tall, with piercing eyes and a full beard, Munele is fierce looking in a compelling kind of way. He is passionate, the kind of guy who would walk a million miles for you and who can kindle minds and hearts as a preacher. The catechists and I prayed with him, each of us asking for God's blessing, and then I anointed him. We all gathered around him, imposing our hands on his head and shoulders and invoking the Spirit of God to heal him. Afterward, he said to us, "I thank you, my brothers. I am sure the Holy Spirit will come to me and heal me from all this. Thank you." Before we left, he and his wife provided us with a meal of bananas and tea. He has lived in this compound in the midst of banana and coconut trees for his nineteen years of exile. Off to the right of my chair was his father's grave and, beyond that, the grave of his mother.

As we were about to leave, I heard Ratib trying to turn the car around on the sandy soil. It turned out our truck's four-wheel drive was not functioning. It took the five of us and several neighbors ninety minutes to get the damn car out of the damn sand, with the village women cheering us on from the sidelines. We used every available tool in our arsenal: big rocks, timbers cannibalized from the roof of a pyot, dry grass, a car jack, banana leaves, hoes, shovels, pangas, and a storehouse of informal knowledge of the laws of physics. Everyone in the village came to talk over the project, emerging from the banana groves like a bank of fog, each person with an angle of attack. Not being skilled in mechanical matters, I offered a few mumbled prayers and acted like I was actually helping when the gang of supervisors was asked to push. At last came the roaring extraction, with Ratib gunning the engine. With one final embrace from Munele, we were out of there. God, how I love that man.

The Feminine Church

When was the last time I saw a chapel full of African nuns? This morning, Sister Joan Atimango asked me to concelebrate Mass at her vow renewal at the Moyo convent of the Sacred Heart, the Sacred Heart sisters' base of operations in northern Uganda and Southern Sudan. I have worked with her in the Adjumani pastoral program since I arrived here, and I was in Moyo because I had stayed overnight for two days of seminars in the Palorinya settlement.

Sister Atimango is in her late twenties. She is tall, like most in her tribe, and outgoing and laughs easily. In addition to her tribal language of Alur, she speaks fluent English and Madi. She is a prayerful woman and loved by the refugee community; the women of the villages plug into her strength and knowledge and wisdom. She is one of them. She works primarily with the young people of the Adjumani Refugee Settlement but does a lot of adult pastoral work in the villages.

She renewed her vows with three others, all Ugandan, all of different tribes: young women recommitting themselves to God, dressed in simple religious attire. Sister Atimango has become one of my best friends and closest confidants. She is never disrespectful of her religious traditions but never gets trapped in formalities, either. She is refreshingly with it, can laugh at herself, and has good instincts for people, including me.

It seems to me that in some parts of the world, the church is not known at all, nor does it want to be known. It is observed and dissected, judged and depicted as little more than a lumbering institution that is out of touch with modernity. I saw a different church at that vow ceremony. Incarnated in those dedicated African women, the church was present to the new, affirming of the future, and a reflection of Christ. I stood in the presence of the church in all its feminine wonder, asserting and blessing what is true and good and vital. And I was aware of the living sacrifice that always exists in the church: here, in a culture that puts such a high premium on women having children, Atimango and her companions take a vow by which they intentionally remove that option from their lives. And they do it not as an act of independence, nor to free themselves from the obligation of loyalty and fruitfulness. Their sacrifice is for the beloved and is embodied in love. Seeing them kneel and take their vows left me with yet another inner icon to carry with me, an icon that reminds me of the church's most sacred commitment to Christ, an icon to which I return often and pay homage.

Keyo

Ratib and I were in Keyo this morning, one of the poorest villages in Palorinya, nestled against one of the rocky ridges that overlook the Nile to the west. We were met there by George Aju, the young catechist, and his wife, who is expecting their first child.

There are no doors on the chapel, so the goats take it over most of the time. Though freshly swept, it still reeked of goat urine. But the people were warm and welcoming. It was a day of baptisms, probably about a dozen babies. The large number, at least by Western standards, is a result of the lack of priests and the large sizes of the families—a function of the people's personal theology, which considers children to be a direct blessing from God. At that particular baptism, the women were dressed in rich greens, purples, and yellows. Translating my words into Madi was Adrian Wani, an intelligent young man who speaks very good English and is handicapped by curvature of the spine. The congregation did a drama based on the story of the thief who comes to raid the sheepfold. Wani played the shepherd—the Good Shepherd—and someone else played the thief.

I reflected during the Mass, as I looked out on everyone, how impossible the scene was to describe. I have been immersed in this world for so long that it all seems so familiar: the smell of goat urine, the faces, the laughter (and sometimes indifference), the strange and mysterious transmission of faith in baptisms and the reading of Scripture, the tribulations of translation, the babies nursing, the effects of malnutrition and lifetimes of hard labor evident on the bodies of the people. Grace has made this African experience so natural for me, unleashing talents that I did not know I had.

One Coin Equals Two Coins

Every Thursday morning, if I have stayed overnight in Moyo for ministry in the Palorinya settlement, there stands at my door a little handicapped woman, Kali by name, probably fifty years old. She speaks only nonsense Madi words, but she can relate. She is usually dressed in the shabbiest of dresses and is always asking me for money. Once, I took a photo of her and gave it to her, and it was like I had given her a precious jewel. When she sees me driving into town, she claps her hands and lets loose with something between a squeal and a giggle.

I usually give her a one-hundred-shilling coin. She always studies it intensely and then races down to the nearest vendor to exchange it for two fifty-shilling coins. I guess the idea is that two is always better than one. I was told that she then carefully packs the money to the local nuns who run an orphanage for infants. Apparently, decades ago, Kali herself was abandoned in front of the convent when she was a baby. She never forgot.

Confirmation and Kalashnikovs

You prepare a table before me
under the eyes of my enemies;
you anoint my head with oil,
my cup brims over.

—Psalm 23:5

I never escape war in the North. It is always in the background: sticky, relentless, and full of horror. Because of periodic raids by the LRA in the southeastern part of the Adjumani settlement, the local government and the commanding officer of the local detachment of the Uganda Peoples' Defense Forces (UPDF) have restricted us from visiting several chapels in the area. But we have been granted permission to go to a couple of the chapels for confirmations. The bishop of Arua is coming to lead the liturgies, and it looks as if we will be bringing with us firepower other than that of the Holy Spirit: the UPDF commander informed Father Idro, the local priest with whom I work in the villages, that we must bring soldiers with us to two of the chapels for extra security.

❋

Idro and I were waved through the security gate at the local UPDF military base. Bishop Drandua drove in last night from Arua and was following in his pickup with a small entourage. Waiting for us were eight soldiers, dressed in camouflage fatigues and carrying Kalashnikov rifles, with extra bullet clips slung around their shoulders. It was odd to be departing for a confirmation with soldiers armed to the teeth sitting and chatting in the bed of the pickup.

We drove an hour to Ibibiaworo; young children met the cars about fifty yards from the chapel and led us in, dancing and singing. It seemed like everyone in the village was there, Catholic and non-Catholic, including a few Muslims who live in a nearby Ugandan village. Once we stopped, the soldiers immediately deployed around the area.

Greeting us and remaining throughout the ceremony was a mentally ill person who periodically gave instructions to anyone who would listen. He was shabbily dressed and grinning from ear to ear as he carried on a dialogue with inner voices, discussing the significance of the situation. He took particular interest in me, alternately smiling and scowling; I presumed it was my whiteness that agitated him. His tasks for the day involved dealing with the unexpected like me and, of course, "assisting" with the confirmation.

The people were extraordinarily tolerant of this man. He was, after all, one of them, so his behavior, though distracting, was nothing harmful. On only a few occasions did an elder walk over to him and gently guide him, hand on elbow, to another location so that he would not be in the way of the proceedings.

Idro, Drandua, and I sat in front of the chapel under UN tarpaulins that the villagers had hung over a large area surrounded by acacia trees. The local women brought us tea and cookies and sent the same to each soldier.

There were fifty confirmation candidates, mostly teenagers and a few adults, from five villages in the settlement. The language of the village is Bari, but the whole ceremony was done in English with periodic Bari translation, and occasionally Arabic. After the Gospel and before the confirmation liturgy, Bishop Drandua gave a brief homily. He is a tall Ugandan from the northwest of the country, a Lugbara by tribe. He clearly loves the people he serves and has been doing so for over fifteen years. He is not a well man, a diabetic, in his sixties. His homily was simple and eloquent. He spoke of the passing on of faith and of both the gift and obligation of being called to follow Christ.

After the homily, the kids stepped forward one by one to be anointed and receive the prayers of the bishop. As he was touching all those young faces, I was reminded of baptism. From the moment we are immersed in the water, we begin to slowly grasp what it means to die into Christ in a sacramental and tangible way and to be incorporated into the church. In confirmation, the Holy Spirit enables us to give witness to the size and power of God's love for the world. As each person was anointed, I prayed for the church of Sudan and that the youth, when they return to their homeland, will be the conduits of God's love.

Surrounded by the barefoot poor, the insane, the weapons of war, and the dust of Uganda's dry season, I asked myself, Is the Holy Spirit really here?

A rhetorical question, I know, O God. You are never limited by place or time, by big or small, by simple or complex. You are not prevented by anything in the exercise of your promise of love manifested in Jesus, most especially in nooks and crannies like Ibibiaworo. Obscurity is your specialty: obscure places, obscure situations, obscure people, obscure bread and wine. Nothing obstructs your grace, O God, not evil, not madness, not the chaos of nations, not the pettiness and grumbling of your servants. Let all of us perceive you anew in these sacred moments. Let every one of these kids be deeply moved. Forever.

There was a great celebration and an abundance of food after the confirmation, and dancing accompanied by drums. The Bari have a peculiar kind of celebratory dance, in which they gather in a circle, and one person enters the circle and proceeds to leap vertically in synch with the circle's clapping and singing. When the central figure tires, he or she stops in front of another person, and that person jumps into the middle of the circle. I can't count the number of times over the years that curious girls and older women have stopped in front of me. Today was no exception. I leaped in. All of the people went crazy, of course. My vertical leap is pitiful, but I'm a hell of a dancer.

※

Today we were at Robidire, the parish center for the Catholics of the Adjumani settlement, twenty-five miles northwest of Ibibiaworo. The bishop, Father Idro, the chapel catechists, and I were seated on a concrete platform outside the chapel. Over two hundred young people, from ten surrounding villages, were to be confirmed. The people love big celebrations, so many were present, including another mentally ill man. Denied immediate access to the action, he stomped off, shaking the dust from his feet, and then, standing at a distance and jabbing a stick into the air for emphasis, he uttered condemnations of the entire event, like some crazed prophet. People who know him and speak the local dialects said that most of what he said was nonsense—all bark and no bite.

We proceeded with the Mass and the confirmation. The bishop spoke as he had in Ibibiaworo and looked into the eyes of each person who came forward to receive the sacrament. I like Bishop Drandua. We have known each other for several years, having first met in the Rhino Camp Refugee Settlement when I was just a rookie in Africa. He is a very pastoral man. Once, when I was working in Rhino, he stopped by the JRS compound to see me; he had heard I was suffering from malaria and knew how terrifying it can be for the inexperienced. He sat down next to my bed, clasped my hand, chatted with me for a while, and gave me a blessing before he left. He is a class act.

How does Drandua maintain a sense of the holy when he does so many of these ceremonies knowing that many of the recipients have only a rudimentary understanding of the ritual's meaning? Back in Adjumani, I asked him this question. "I have been nourished by my position," he told me, "just as surely as the faithful are nourished by me. I believe that the Spirit is constantly renewing the church; it is a river which cannot be dammed. So the Spirit renews the bishops." He paused and added, "If they are open." His reflection was as powerful in its simplicity as it was in its theology. Drandua's conviction that the Spirit renews the church, now and forever, educated or uneducated, stands strong in its truth. Maybe that is the convert in me talking. God will not abandon the church and it will always grow, if not in numbers, then in the quality of love found in its members and in its capacity to be renewed and transformed by the Holy Spirit.

My God, the obstacles that man faces, the immensity of the distances he must travel, the challenges to an emerging Christianity that he must confront. But he takes them on.

☀

We took UPDF soldiers with us to the village of Elema, northeast of Robidire. Again, because of the crowds, we could not have the confirmation in the chapel, so it was held under a huge neem tree on the grounds of the Melijo grade school. The people were joyous, spontaneously dancing and singing when the bishop exited his truck. Almost one hundred children were confirmed.

Drandua gave the homily in his native Lugbara, since most there were of the Madi tribe, one that understands his mother tongue. There was a moment during the Mass, as the bishop was elevating the chalice, when I saw, off in the distance, the deployed soldiers moving on the perimeter of the confirmation site. They were packing Kalashnikovs capable of firing six hundred rounds per minute. It was a crazy juxtaposition.

Elema put on a great show after the ceremony. The bishop always likes a beer if it can be had, and after the liturgy one appeared for him, and one for me too. The kids acted out a hilarious drama in which they turned some social dynamics on their head. For example, there was a depiction of a drunk man stumbling home and receiving a beating from his wife, not vice versa. The women in the crowd howled, as did the children. Some men in the crowd glared disapprovingly, while others had a good laugh. On a deeper level, the scene spoke to the fact that women here, who are traditionally viewed as a mat to be stepped on, are becoming more and more assertive as wives and mothers.

Finally, the village presented Drandua with gifts: a hundred-pound bag of maize, two goats, and a sheep. It is the custom also for each village to give a small amount of money for his fuel.

The first thing that strikes me when I am among the Dinka tribe is that they are very tall—and I'm a tall guy. Today we were in a refugee village composed of Dinkas, who, in addition to being tall, are gracious, self-possessed, persistent in goals, and—I am told—utterly fearless in battle.

We arrived at Mirieyi at ten in the morning; it was the last day of confirmations. Another large crowd had gathered, with over one hundred to be confirmed. The bishop was tired, so he sat down for the anointing today. Since we were in a secure area, near the town of Adjumani, there was no need for soldiers. I decided that if the LRA were to interfere with a Dinka ceremony of any kind, especially one at which guests were present, and even more if priests were present, the Dinkas would chase them all the way to Cairo if necessary, and no prisoners would be taken.

What was most interesting about the confirmation visit to Mirieyi, besides the simple music of drums and the unfeigned piety of the Dinkas, was the long post-confirmation program. It included an extremely funny drama, in which a sick person was attended to first by a crazed, palsied witch doctor and then by a group of Christians. The witch doctor, whose face was made up with fat eyebrows and a huge bushy mustache, demanded money from the sick man and then failed to cure his illness. Then the Christians came and prayed over the sick man, and he was healed. He rose from his mat, and the crowd cheered, much to the frustration of the witch doctor (a great actor).

After the drama, the Dinka women performed a spectacular dance. I have been to this chapel many times, and rarely have I seen more than a handful of women. Public prayers, liturgical music, and the celebration of the Eucharist are primarily the job of the men and boys; the women's religious practice takes place more in the home. The women's dance was hypnotizing, and I watched with mouth wide, like someone from the plains seeing his first mountain. It happened like this: about twenty women gathered in a circle, all of them stately, handsome, and wearing brilliant multicolored dresses. Then three women entered the circle. The entire group began a rhythmic song that built to rapid-fire clapping around the circle and feet stomping by those inside, in unison with the clapping. The dancers inside the circle threw back their shoulders and lifted their arms high and back, as if they were reaching for something behind them. They held their heads high, proud and strong, their eyes closed. Then they fell to their knees and proceeded to move around in the circle, keeping the cadence and pulse of their surrounding sisters. After a few minutes, the three in the circle left, and three more took their place. To see the energy pouring out of them was breathtaking. I was told that this dance was not often done for outsiders, only special guests. What a gift.

After the entertainment, the Dinkas served rice and bread and tea—and a beer for the bishop. Gifts were given to him also: huge sacks of beans, more goats, and a large number of chickens. Drandua, Idro, and I left to the clapping and ululating of all.

That night, back at the residence of Idro's community, the Apostles of Jesus, there was a dinner for the bishop. It was a quiet night, such a contrast to the celebrations of the week. I felt honored to have been a part of and a witness to that expression of the heart of the African Church. Many images ricocheted around in my head and heart: the truck loaded with troops; the colorful clothes and spontaneous dancing of the women; hundreds of young people being anointed; curious children gathered around me. And, too, I recalled the evident piety of the people in the villages, the tradition of the faith incarnated in the African bishop, and the feel of eyes and hands upon me, those of people who love and cherish me for walking with them in exile.

Letter from Nimule, Sudan

Dear V.,

I have come to Sudan to spend New Year's with a JRS friend. Happy New Year. I hope this finds you and yours well. I prayed for you especially on Christmas Eve, when I celebrated Mass in a village called Alere, and on Christmas Day, in the village of Esia. One of the Esia children had been given a pair of shoes for Christmas that squeaked when he walked. I suppose they came over in one of those huge bales of clothes that are shipped into refugee village markets and sold for a song. It was hilarious watching him—and hearing him—move around the chapel, checking things out.

The people responded enthusiastically to the homily, based on a drama I had cooked up in which people in the congregation played the holy family. The people gave powerful responses to my questions, their answers rooted not in doctrine but in their personal relationship with God. They made the connection quickly between themselves and Mary and Joseph and Jesus: on the move, on the run. There were children in the audience whose Madi name in English is "Flight," like flight in the night from a killing enemy—and, from the parents' perspective, successful flight, because of God's providence. All the people applauded after the drama and homily, and they applauded again at the end of Mass when I wished them a blessed Christmas and told them I hoped the next one would be in Sudan.

As the people were applauding, I reflected on a seminal moment in the life of Archbishop Oscar Romero. During his passionate oration at the funeral of the Jesuit Rutilio Grande, his close friend who had been murdered by the Salvadoran military, Romero's people cheered and praised him. One commentator said that at that moment, Romero experienced another kind of baptism. The observer wrote that "there is a baptism of water and there is a baptism of blood and then there is the baptism of the people."

I am baptized constantly in Uganda.

You asked how the teaching is going. As I move through the villages, I am probably saying the same thing only in different ways, depending on the makeup of the congregation and the atmosphere in the chapel. In essence, I am teaching about the loving heart of God, and I seek to communicate that truth to the many catechists given to me—and they in turn share with me what they learn. So I am teaching teachers how to teach their faith.

How do I communicate in the bush with all my leadership? Good question. In this world, there are no telephones (I have a cell phone, but my people do not), no fax machines, and no Batman signals in the night sky. So communication is a challenge. I usually plan with the leaders three months in advance and make a schedule that is distributed to all the people and chapels involved by leaders who travel by bike from village to village. Miraculously, when I arrive at a particular village chapel for a seminar, the leaders and their people are there, from fifteen to two hundred strong. Often the weather is hot or rainy and most of the people have not had a decent meal—if any meal—but all are ready to jump into a seminar on church life. Their attitude leaves me scratching my head and humming inside. With all their suffering and deprivation, the refugees are eager and hungry to learn and talk about faith.

When we finish our seminars, we have tea and gab, and the little children gather around me and stare and giggle. Most of the children love to come close, but some younger ones fear me and cry because I look so hideous. Teasing older brothers and sisters utter those hair-raising words: "Be good and stop crying or the *cawaja* will eat you."

Last week, I celebrated Sunday Mass at a wretchedly poor village, Baratuku, located in rocky and dry terrain maybe four miles from the Nile. Mass was held underneath a tree; the congregation used to have a thatched chapel, but the termites finally chewed it down. I pulled up in the pickup, and only an old man and his wheelchair-bound nineteen-year-old daughter, suffering from what I guessed was cerebral palsy, were present. Smiling crookedly at me, she made a mighty effort to clap a welcome. The University of Oregon's marching band, in all its regalia, could not have topped the greeting.

November was a busy and strange month. The director of the JRS project in Adjumani had to attend meetings in Europe for a month, so I directed the operation while he was gone. The project has many pans in the fire. I signed a lot of checks, attended NGO meetings, and sorted out a few personnel problems. In the meantime, I was still going to five villages a week, conducting seminars for leadership and celebrating Mass and addressing the pastoral needs of the people. Lots of traveling, lots of people, lots of death, lots of problems (flat tires, bad communication, delayed ferries, sick leaders). Plus, throughout the month I was afflicted with a litany of illnesses, including a bad bout of malaria and a pesky allergy. And two days ago, while hanging clothes, I was bitten on my toes by tiny brown ants called "oboleebos," causing my feet to puff up. I guess it all comes with the turf. I will be happy to see the director, my German brother Frido, return from Europe.

Know I think of you and pray for you. I love you ten thousand elephants and a million hippos.

Hope you are well and not too busy. Take care of yourself.

Love,

Gary

Holding Job in My Arms

Ah, would that these words of mine were written down,
  inscribed on some monument
with iron chisel and engraving tool,
  cut into the rock for ever.
This I know: that my Avenger lives,
  and he, the Last, will take his stand on earth.
After my awaking, he will set me close to him,
  and from my flesh I shall look on God.

—Job 19:23–26

Ratib, my driver, and I left Adjumani around seven this morning and headed for the Palorinya settlement village of Morobi. The Nile was quiet, dotted with small floating islands of hyacinth and papyrus, as the ferry moved across it. We do this once a week, Ratib and I, going over for a day of ministry in one village, staying the night, and going to another village the next day, making our way back late in the afternoon. Once we got off the ferry, we drove two hours on the rocky roads of Palorinya, picking up along the way Virgilio Lodu, the catechist of Orinya, and later Matilde Eiyo, the catechist of Dongo. They would help me with counsel, translation, and teaching.

As we traveled toward Morobi, Lodu informed me that Flabius, the head catechist in the village, had lost a daughter, and she had been buried only the day before. "He probably will not be at the seminar, Father, because there is much grief. This was his only child."

But it was a much deeper tragedy. This good man had lost not only his twenty-one-year-old daughter, and his wife a few years ago, but over time seven children to war and disease. Four died in Sudan at the hands of government soldiers as his family was fleeing the hostilities in the mid-nineties, and three died in Morobi of malaria. As for this last child, Sabina, the cause of death was unknown. She became ill and died within twenty-four hours. This happens in the bush: one day a person appears healthy, able to perform the physical tasks in the village and the home, and the next day she is gone, her body struck down by a swift and efficient killer. In the far reaches of the Ugandan bush, an autopsy to determine the specific cause of death is not possible, so the deceased is typically buried swiftly. As is the custom, Sabina was buried adjacent to Flabius's tukul, next to the graves of his wife and Sabina's three siblings who had died in Uganda.

At the Morobi chapel—a table and a few log benches under a huge tree—we were greeted by a group of young Nuer men. It was an uncharacteristically subdued greeting, a sign of respect for their catechist, who, although he is Bari, speaks fluent Arabic, a second language of the Nuer. The Nuer, cousins of the Dinkas, are tall and, in the case of the men, frequently marked on their foreheads with ritual scars, a sign of their tribe and their coming of age. Like the Dinkas, the Nuer place liturgical responsibilities in the hands of the men, although this village has a preponderance of Bari, whose women, in a tribal custom opposite that of the Nuer, lead the Prayers. At a Mass in Morobi, the Nuer men and the Bari women share responsibilities for singing. The Nuer use only an accompanying hand drum, and the Bari use handmade stringed instruments.

There were small children everywhere. I always bring along a little hand puppet, Scovia, a gift from a friend in the States. As I unpacked, I slowly brought her out of my backpack, her big-eared, big-eyed, smiling face on my hand. I had her look around, and the kids clapped their hands in delight.

At one point during the seminar, Flabius appeared and took a seat off to my left. He is a frail, gray-haired man of about fifty, small of stature, with a face dominated by huge gleaming eyes. He is soft-spoken, kind, and respected by his people for his wisdom, which is born, I am sure, of years of suffering and deep faith. Catechists receive no money for their work; they serve their people selflessly in a million pastoral ways from birth to death. In Africa, they are the heart of the day-to-day Catholic Church, the tall trees of faith. They serve out of a deep sense of commitment to and love for their people and an unyielding confidence in God. I was astonished that Flabius was there, given the devastation he must have been going through. I interrupted what I was saying, went over to him, greeted him with the traditional handshake, and put my arms around him. I held his head to my heart and in Arabic whispered into his ear, "I am sorry, my brother, I am sorry."

I thought to myself: *My God, I'm holding Job in my arms.*

We proceeded with the seminar, in which we were presenting theology and Scripture related to the seasons of the church year. It was nothing fancy or profound, but an effort to help the people gain a bigger picture of their Sunday Prayers and, too, understand their faith better. There were lots of questions and answers, and dramas to illustrate various points. People looked to Flabius periodically, in part out of concern and in part seeking his approval of the teaching. He nodded thoughtfully. Off to my left, the children maintained their vigil; in front of me, the men sat on one side of the chapel and the women on the other. I was told that there were over three hundred people present.

In the Mass after the seminar, I did a little drama for the homily, with Lodu translating into Arabic. It was about the notion of gift, building on what I think are the relentless gifts of God's heart: Christ's life and death and resurrection, and the Holy Spirit, and the love that prompts the act of redemption. I took half a loaf of bread and started to eat it, informing everyone that I had not eaten in two days and was therefore very hungry. But then, acting, I looked around at the people hungrier than I was: children, nursing mothers, old men and women, some handicapped people—all of these, I said, had been without nourishment longer than I had. So I gave several people a piece of the bread until all of it had been distributed, and I was left with nothing.

I asked the people, "What have I done?" There were many responses, but the people all understood the main idea: the giver gives because he loves the receiver. My bread is your bread, a gift of love. I pointed to Flabius and said that this was what he had done for years for his community and his family. The people nodded in agreement. At the conclusion of the liturgy, I asked Flabius to say the final prayer. We stood together, holding hands, as he prayed.

There was a meal for us after the seminar and Mass, a modest one of beans and bread, offered in a small meeting tukul connected to the chapel. Lodu, Eiyo, and I had taught for about four hours. Several elders were in attendance. When the meal was over, Flabius, who had sat silently while we ate, asked to say a few words. Speaking in his native Bari, with Eiyo translating, he said something like this:

> I don't have much to say, Father and my brothers and
> sisters. I have suffered deeply this past week with the death
> of my last child, and now I am alone, and there is no one
> to assist me, except yourselves, for which I am grateful. I
> did not feel like coming to Prayers today, but I needed to

trust God, and to come and give to him all my pain, and trust that the Word of God will heal me in these trying times. I came because God is great and his plans, though hidden from us, are plans of love for all of us. I am here with you knowing that being with my brothers and sisters and you, Father Gary, I shall be given strength.

We sat in silence for a long time, letting the rain of his words soak into the soil of our hearts. He concluded, his heavy eyes catching us all in a single glance, "I don't have much more to say. Pray for me and thank you."

It was heartbreaking. There were seven men and two women in that tukul, and each one knew his or her own version of that dear man's agony. They too had lost children; they too had seen death slash into their lives and raid them in the night and in the day, stealing precious pieces of their hearts. This is part of the landscape of the refugee's life. But none there had lost *eight* children. Has any parent lost eight children, anywhere?

The circle of people around Flabius looked up at him with one empathetic face. Words were not necessary. Flabius knew that all were grieving with him. I was struck by the purity of this exchange between a human being and his brothers and sisters, the utter honesty of the moment, the transparency of the human spirit on display. I was witnessing the Body of Christ suffering and ministering simultaneously. At times, Christ is available to us only in the unyielding love and honesty found in the hands and hearts of the people of our community. This has got to be the idea behind that haunting expression in Matthew 25: "Just as you did it to one of the least of these who are members of my family, you did it to me" (NRSV). I found Jesus that day in that consummately obscure place with my companions, those least of my brothers and sisters.

Lodu said a final prayer of thanksgiving. I embraced brother Flabius one more time.

We moved toward the pickup, and the children danced us out, several of the braver little ones running ahead of us as we pulled away—they moved slowly so that we would remain longer in their presence. Looking back past all the waving hands and shining faces, I saw Flabius, standing to the left and in the back of the crowd, bidding us farewell with a peaceful smile and a gentle wave. Behind him stood two watchful Nuer men, looking after their suffering Bari brother.

Kogwon Narju

Each day here takes me into new experiences, deeper experiences, yet linking me with the past. I am an old tree growing steadily but always with a new growth of leaves and blossoms. Grace and love move in my heart, and each place and event becomes a new sanctuary of the mystery of my faith.

Yesterday I traveled to the west side of the Nile with Ratib to do a one-day seminar in the settlement village of Cochi. When we arrived, after two hours of driving in the rain and ferry delays, I talked strategy and plans for the seminar with my lead catechists, Kenyi and Osura, as people were coming into the chapel. Nearly a hundred people were there.

It is Lent, so I focused on the theology of the season and how it fits into the church year. That led into a discussion of the life of Christ and why God even bothered to send his Son. What, I asked, is the point of Jesus' suffering and dying for us? In these seminars, I use Scripture and lots of acting to engage the group as much as I can in a dialogue about our topic. I know that they have the truth within them. My job is to tease it out and help them claim it.

We were at it for more than three hours.

At the heart of the teaching was the fact that we sin and are forgiven and loved by the one who creates us, the one who sent his only Son as the promise of his love and forgiveness. We are loved sinners.

I asked everyone: "Well, what is sin?"

They gave a variety of answers: "murder," "adultery," "gossip," "stealing," "selfishness," "hate," "not being faithful to God."

"Are we are all sinners?"

The congregation, in a convinced chorus: "Yes, all are sinners."

I pointed to a man in the front row. "Even this old man here?"

"Yes, all are sinners."

"Even this beautiful young mother and her child?"

"Yes, all."

"But surely not Kenyi, your good and holy catechist?"

Lots of nodding and laughs. "Yes, all." (Kenyi cracked up as I shook my head at him in mock disapproval.)

"But surely not me, the priest? A sinner?"

Now there were lots of snorts, and a chorus of "You, too!" I acted hurt. More laughing from the congregation.

Then I asked, "Did Jesus tell us any stories about how God forgives our sins and loves us in spite of our sin?"

There was hesitation, and then a hand went up: "Yes, the prodigal son."

"Could you tell us that story?"

The woman stood up and utterly nailed the parable; she was animated, capturing all the attendant emotions and convictions of the story. I asked her to come forward to play the role of the parent of the child who spends his inheritance and then returns to fall on his parent's mercy. She was a frail-looking woman, maybe forty-five, wearing a colorful green and black headpiece. Another person was chosen to be the wayward child, and they acted out the moment of the boy's return after blowing all his inheritance in Kampala. The son fell on his knees, begging forgiveness from his mother. She picked him up and embraced him, showing unconditional acceptance of her son.

> While he was still a long way off, his father saw him and
> was moved with pity. He ran to the boy, clasped him in his
> arms and kissed him tenderly. (Luke 15:20)

To the woman, I said: "Why did you forgive your boy?"

She responded, "Well, he is my son. I must welcome him and forgive him."

"But *why* must you forgive your son?"

From the back of the chapel, an old woman exclaimed, "Kogwon narju!" It is Bari for "Because of love!"—the ultimate explanation of the mother's act and of the Incarnation. The mother in the drama nodded her head in agreement. So did I.

To the boy, I asked: "Why did your mother forgive you?"

"Because I am her son."

"But you are a selfish and greedy son."

"But she loves me."

I kneaded this truth; Kenyi was pacing me now, figurative fingers on the pulse of my heart, seamlessly tying together in Bari my theology and rhetoric.

I instructed the actors to sit down; everyone present applauded. Then I asked a man and a woman in the chapel, Mawa and Josephina, both parents, to come up.

I asked Josephina: "Would you buy exercise books for your daughter who needs them for school?"

"Yes."

"Why?"

"I want her to have the right materials so she can finish school."

"Why?"

"Kogwon narju—because I love her."

I turned to Mawa and asked the same question.

"Yes," he said, for the same reason.

I said to everyone in the chapel: "Now remember, we are trying to understand how much God loves us."

Then I said to Mawa: "Your daughter has to go to Kampala for a medical procedure. Will you raise the money so she can go, and so you can go with her?" Such a trip costs forty dollars in this land where one dollar is a fortune.

"Yes, if I can, I will do everything in my power."

"Why?"

"Because I love her."

When I asked Josephina the same question, she didn't miss a beat: "I will cut firewood and sell grain and borrow from friends so that she can go."

"Why?"

Before she could answer, I turned to the congregation, listening intently, and asked them for the answer.

In a single voice they responded: "Kogwon narju."

I turned to Josephina again: "And if the doctor says your child's kidneys are failing, but she can be saved by a transplant of one of your kidneys—a serious operation in which she will probably live and you might die—would you do it? Would you give one of your kidneys?" (Everyone in the chapel was gripped now, leaning forward, trying to answer the question for themselves.)

"Yes," Josephina answered firmly. "I have lived my life"—said this woman in her early thirties—"and my daughter deserves to live." Smiles, nods, and sighs from the people.

"Why would you do this?"

"I love her. Kogwon narju."

Now I asked Mawa what he would do.

He hesitated, then said, "I have two other girls; if I die, who would provide for them? Perhaps it is best that my daughter die." In a flash I was thinking of all the families I have known in three different refugee settlements who have lost at least one child, some five or six or seven.

"And if the doctor says you will not die if you donate one of your kidneys?"

"Then I will gladly give one of my kidneys."

"Why?"

"Kogwon narju."

I asked them to sit down. The chapel was buzzing. It was a good drama, but it was not over.

The next question I posed to all. "Suppose a doctor comes to you and is trying to find a volunteer for a kidney transplant for a sick person in the village. You look like a possibility as a donor. The person will die without a transplant, and in giving your kidney you may die. Would you do it?"

Someone in the back asked: "Who is it?"

I answered slowly, "It is your worst enemy."

Silence.

Then lots of head shaking, nervous laughter, bewildered looks; an old man in the back walked out, waving his arms as if to say, "This is crazy talk." Kenyi laughed as he translated the gentleman; I think he softened it for me. But the old man returned, interested to know what people would say. A mother, nursing her baby directly in front of me, couldn't stop laughing. There were lots of puzzled looks as the people sunk their teeth into the question.

The hands started to go up.

"No way."

"Never for my enemy."

"I would give my kidney. Jesus died for his enemies; am I his follower or not?"

"Humanly, this is impossible. Perhaps with the grace of God, but who has that grace?"

"How is it possible to love this person if in our death our dependents will be without us?"

The chapel was abuzz; everyone was talking—to themselves, to me, to their neighbor, to God—a hundred people engaging their faith, engaging the spirit of God's heart. I reminded them of our question: How great is God's love?

After much discussion, we concluded the seminar. Kenyi and Osura took everyone through a recap of the day's teaching in Bari, with no English to obstruct things. Then they asked the people for an evaluation of the day. They were unanimous: this has been good teaching; we must do it again.

As we left, happiness moved across my heart like the Nile's morning breeze over my face. It was stiflingly hot, I was tired and hungry, the trip ahead would be long and bumpy, I was surrounded by so much poverty—yet I was filled with consolation. It can't be just joy at a job well done. Is it not the joy of the Spirit in me, the joy of God in me?

Ratib smiled reflectively as he downshifted over the last difficult terrain to the main road. He was happy that the day had gone well and that the people were appreciative. Ratib, a Muslim, is my biggest fan.

African Gem

I can get down and circle depression at times. I suppose that is because of a diet that includes unresolved wars, government corruption, the death of children, niggling tropical illnesses, and periodic snafus in programs and personnel conflicts. But there are good things as well, and the morning star trumps the dark star.

One example is Pamela. When I met her, she was fourteen. I spotted her as I came in from one of the villages; she was sitting in front of the JRS offices, among the waiting crowd of people, most of them students. She looked vaguely familiar. I came out of the office a few hours later, and she was still there, sitting under a huge mango tree that shadows the office. One of the staff had noticed her too and observed that she seemed abnormally passive, approaching no one. I went over to her.

"Do I know you?" I asked.

"Yes," she responded. "I am called Pamela, and we met a few years ago when you worked in the Rhino Camp Refugee Settlement. I was very small then, one of the dancers at Mass."

"You are a long way from Rhino," I said. "Why are you here, why the long wait?"

"I was told that JRS sponsors girls in the secondary schools of Adjumani. I have waited because I was fearing to talk to anyone."

"And how did you get here?"

"I walked."

Did she ever. Rhino Camp Refugee Settlement is sixty miles by road and probably fifty by shortcuts. It is a tough three-day trip by foot through the bush. Family pressure and the prospect of an empty future in her village had brought her to Adjumani. Her one clear desire was an education. She had finished primary school and wanted to attend secondary school. She dreamed that she would have a chance in the North, in a JRS secondary school in Adjumani. The alternative was to stay in her village and be married off by her grandmother (her parents are dead) to an interested uncle.

Pamela left Rhino with one thousand Ugandan shillings (about fifty cents).

JRS in Adjumani assists in the education of thousands of Sudanese children in nursery, primary, and secondary schools. Secondary school students leave their villages to attend one of the central schools in the Adjumani and Palorinya settlements. The schools are administered by JRS but are under the authority of the Ugandan education system. Students board at the refugee secondary schools, as secondary school students do throughout Uganda. If they are high achievers in primary school, refugee students can receive financial assistance from UNHCR to attend secondary schools in larger Ugandan towns where facilities are better and the teaching staff is more experienced and better paid.

The secondary school facilities in the refugee settlements are meager. They have no running water, no electricity, no kitchens, and no dining halls. The kids live in dormitories or in small, one-room tukuls on the school property. There are never enough textbooks. Teachers are dedicated but underpaid.

Students in Uganda must pay fees for each of the school year's three terms. In the refugee settlements of Adjumani and Palorinya, each term costs about twenty thousand shillings, or about ten dollars. In expensive urban schools, yearly fees can be millions of shillings. In addition to school fees, our refugees must find money for food (the schools provide a simple lunch, but other meals are up to the student), mosquito nets, soap, a change of clothes, shoes, a portable mattress, writing paper, pens, and a kerosene lamp. Girls have the additional expenses of feminine hygiene products. For most refugee students, because they are poor and frequently have lost immediate family, money is a constant struggle. This is evident at the start of every new term, when hundreds of students come to the JRS offices seeking assistance.

From this American's point of view, the amount sought is a drop in the bucket. But therein lies the cruel truth of inequality: fee money is not, nor ever will be, a drop in the bucket for the refugee, especially the female refugee. It is an ocean. The cost of one term, plus additional expenses, at the JRS-administered secondary school in Adjumani is less than that of a dinner out with a friend or a bottle of wine or a night at the movies in the States, or a Christmas present for a child, or half a tank of gas, or a magazine subscription. It is always painful to see the consumption in the West—all that money spent on so many trivial things and pursuits—and know that here kids face a challenge akin to climbing Mount Everest in their efforts to raise money for education. Without sponsors, they can't even get to base camp. All these refugee children want is an education. Just that.

Heading north, taking a shortcut along the west side of the Nile, Pamela came to the village of Lebongi at the end of her first day of walking. She was traveling in the dry season, so it was hot, and the dust clung to her like a fever. She had her dinner at Lebongi: a bag of peanuts that cost her one hundred shillings. People at the village borehole gave her some water to drink. She slept that night on a dirt floor in an open church. The next day, for eight hundred shillings, she secured a motorboat ride across the Nile. Arriving on the east side of the river, she asked directions to Adjumani and started walking northeast. As she told her story to me, I thought of the old folk song "Follow the Drinking Gourd," sung by slaves fleeing the pre–Civil War South. Its words speak of traveling by night, following the Big Dipper. Pamela's heart was her Big Dipper.

On the second night, she slept again in a church, in a village called Maaji, an area infested with units of the LRA. For her evening meal, Pamela spent her last one hundred shillings for a few bananas. On the third day, in mid-afternoon, she arrived at Adjumani, the last major northern Ugandan town on the east side of the Nile. She walked this day without food. Adjumani has three main streets that are usually jammed with people and bicycles. The JRS office is located at the end of one of them. When Pamela reached her destination, she rested under the shade of the mango tree.

After we talked, I brought her to the project director, Father Frido Pflueger, a smiling German Jesuit. Before he came to Uganda, he was the headmaster of an exceptional secondary school in Dresden. I asked Pamela to repeat her story to him. Her face reflected anxiety, sadness, and fear, but also determination, hope, and anticipation.

As they talked, it was even more evident how bright and articulate she was. In addition to her mother tongue of Kakwa, she spoke excellent English and fluent Arabic. She made her case to Pflueger, utterly convinced that she was to be there and that God, who had brought her, would provide for her. I kept saying to myself: *My God, she's only a kid.* She had nothing but a small book in a plastic bag and the clothes she wore. She had no money—not a shilling.

Pflueger asked, "Do you have any records, Pamela?"

"Yes, I have the results of my final year, in Primary Seven; my refugee ID card; my refugee ration card; and a letter from a Rhino Camp government official that affirms that I am a refugee."

She carried all these documents tucked inside a beat-up Primary Five mathematics book, which she carried in an equally beat-up black plastic bag. She carefully removed the book from the bag, as if it was a fragile and ancient relic passed on to her for safekeeping.

One significant aspect of the JRS effort here is an affirmative-action program that encourages the female child to continue school. Through the program, we pay a part of each female student's school fees and distribute free menstrual pads, soap, washing materials, and underwear.

In many African cultures, girls are seen as inferior. Where money is tight—and it almost always is—boys are given preference over girls in terms of who receives an education, because boys are considered more capable academically. Girls are a future investment for a family, because they will be married off for a dowry. As girls grow up, they are expected to perform many duties: cooking, cleaning, babysitting younger siblings, collecting water and firewood, digging and planting, and harvesting for food. School can get in the way of these duties.

When parents are agreeable to their daughter having an education, there often remains the problem of safe and suitable accommodations at the schools. And, too, if a girl does not have access to sanitary materials and underwear during menstruation, it can result in her missing an inordinate number of days every month, and it becomes increasingly difficult for her to catch up. But the alternative is often worse: uneducated and reaching childbearing age, a girl is married off, and once she starts having children, her chance at an education is lost. So education can be a way up and out—a chance.

Eventually, with Pflueger's help, Pamela was admitted to a local JRS-administered facility, Alere Secondary School. She paid her fees through the financial assistance of anonymous European donors who provide for such eventualities under Pflueger's supervision. My pastoral team was able to raise extra money to cover her material needs.

On the day she received her admissions papers, Pamela came to the JRS office to chat. She was beaming.

"Are you happy, Pamela?" I asked her.

"Yes, I am very happy."

"Were you ever afraid of making the trip alone?"

"Yes, often, but I knew that this is what I wanted to do, and I trusted in God."

"But you are now in a new school where there are many strangers and many different tribes. Some kids will probably have more money than you."

"Doesn't matter. God has given me a chance. Those things are insignificant."

In my carefree high school days, all I had to worry about was earning high grades in unchallenging classes and scoring points for the basketball team. It was nothing compared to Pamela's struggle for an education. There are many like her, African gems. Most of their stories are not as dramatic, but each one inspires the day-to-day educational work of the JRS, which helps individuals gain a toehold in a cultural system that can hijack personal aspirations in the name of traditional prerogatives. Pamela's is just one story of a girl's determination to climb the mountain and cross to the other side rather than terminate the journey because of anticipated—and very real—hardships.

Periodically she comes by, and if I'm at the office we go sit under the mango tree. We talk as daughter to father, as student to teacher, and as friend to friend.

Letter from Kampala

Dear M.,

I write this from Kampala, where I have come for a break. I needed a week to slow down and lick a few wounds. It is revitalizing to step back from the tensions and demands of the North. I must have spent fifteen minutes under a hot shower at the Jesuit residence on my first morning.

Imaginary conversation of the Kampala Jesuits:

Jesuit # 1: What in the hell happened to all the hot water?
Jesuit # 2: Hmm. Is Gary Smith here?

He sure is. Other acts of depravity: eating cheese and crackers with a bottle of wine, downing several apples, and consuming—in a single sitting—one large Snickers bar.

It looks like peace between the North and the South in Sudan will come soon, so over the next few years the refugees will be heading back home, if all the right circumstances are in place. For example, most are without transportation, so they have to wait for the UNHCR to provide a ride; the secondary education in Southern Sudan is lacking, so many people will remain in Uganda to ensure that their teenagers receive a decent education; drought and famine will keep most here for the time, because there is not enough food for even a short journey; and many of the roads in Southern Sudan still have to be stripped of mines. And recent attacks by the LRA in Sudan, where they have base camps, make the decision to return even more complicated. Yet some have returned. As the crow flies, it is not a long way.

Even though the LRA fools have not hit Adjumani in a few years, one is always aware of its potential for creating havoc. Last Sunday, a few of us stopped off at a café for a dinner of rice and beans. Parked in front of the place was a huge South African–made armored personnel carrier called a Mamba, bristling with stony-faced Ugandan soldiers and their weapons. Ah, nothing like a quiet evening out for dinner with friends.

The rainy season is upon us. Some days, driving east into the Nile valley and toward the ferry at Laropi, heading home, I am treated to a breathtaking panorama. I see clouds as big as cities, so I give them names like Los Angeles and Kinshasa. The rains bring a new burst of life. In our compound, the trees—avocado, mango, jackfruit, guava, lemon, moringa, jacaranda, acacia, papaya, and neem—are making their move, most having survived the dry season. But the change of weather can be a Trojan horse, since mosquitoes can reproduce fast in the cooler temperatures.

As I look back over my months here, one obvious reflection is that my world has been turned around, and my ways of seeing and thinking have been jarred loose and recast. I have been faced with a legion of cultural adjustments and confronted with my own personal strengths and demons. I remember plowing through a field of dandelions one spring day in Winnipeg, sending dandelion parachutes everywhere, dislodged from the safety of the mother dandelion and landing in new ground with new surroundings and new challenges to survival. I feel like that. I have been knocked loose—hurled sometimes. Old ways of relating don't work here, and a new level of sensitivity emerges. I am still the same guy but replanted in the daily vicissitudes of the culture and environment of Africa. And that culture has brought me much that is new and fresh, although sometimes devastating.

Africa is in pathetic shape: wars, thugs running governments, AIDS, unforgiving poverty, disease, malnutrition—there is so much that is bad and depressing. But Africa's people are rich in life and humor and faith and courage, the stuff that is born of difficult, volatile situations, like a glazed piece of pottery coming alive in the heat of a kiln. One cannot help but be touched—and changed—by all this. And God's love is in that touch and change. Sometimes I feel like I have been here for centuries, and each day takes me deeper and deeper and further and further into who I am and what I believe.

I keep you and your writing in my prayers.

I love you.

Gary

God Does Not Forget
His People

You who live in the shelter of the Most High,
who abide in the shadow of the Almighty,
will say to the LORD, "My refuge and my fortress;
my God, in whom I trust."
For he will deliver you from the snare of the fowler
and from the deadly pestilence;
he will cover you with his pinions,
and under his wings you will find refuge.

—Psalm 91:1–4, NRSV

In the Sudanese refugee experience, there is a poignant analogy to the Jewish experience. The Israelites were formed by their miraculous deliverance from the pursuing enemy and their harsh desert exodus. Their awareness of God was made personal by God's intervention in the seemingly endless, chaotic journey out of the Sinai wilderness. In the same way, many Sudanese refugees' experience of God began with the terrifying trip out of Sudan and the journey to Uganda. Like the Israelites, they lived to tell about the escape and to share it with their children.

In our experience of God and grace, there are transforming moments. Sometimes they are explosive, turning our life upside down, and sometimes they begin and endure over a long period of time, leaving us, in the end, with a profound interior change. Whatever the transformation, swift or gradual, life is never the same. Critics can disdain the faith experience, and write it off as a delusion of grandeur, but for those who have experienced God in peril, the encounter is true and undeniable. They can point to their lives as evidence of it, like the blind man in the Gospel of John: "I only know that I was blind and now I can see" (9:25).

What follows are brief interviews with Sudanese refugees. Almost to a person, they begin the description of their experience of God not with their morning prayers, but with those traumatic, tragedy-filled days of escape from Sudan. It is an experience, incidentally, that illuminates and informs those morning prayers.

Charles, 32

I fled from Kajo Keji several years ago. It is there that my awareness—my real awareness—of God began. I moved in the bush, avoiding both what looked like government soldiers and soldiers of the Sudan People's Liberation Army. I was traveling alone; my family had been killed. All of them. I believe that God led me to safety. I do not understand why I was not killed or why I did not starve to death; I only know at some point I turned to God and told him that I trusted him and that I was in his hands.

Here in Uganda, I experience God in people as they live the gospel. What I mean is that people love each other and stay together at a time when things are very difficult: lack of work, sickness, insufficient food, the loss of close loved ones. The community helps me believe. And I know God is present by the moral support that people give to us, as, for example, the priests of JRS and the Comboni Fathers. These are people who come to share our suffering and to share spiritual gifts that they may have. It is like God is saying through them, "I did not abandon you when you came away from your homeland; now I will not abandon you in exile. I will send others to love you and teach you of my concern."

Virgilio, 41

I never expected to reach here. In our flight from Juba, I was captured by the government army, tortured, received no medical care, and then escaped and rejoined my family.

One of my children was delivered on the way and lived; we were cold in our travels, but God cared for us and got us here—somehow. And once we arrived in Uganda and were settled in the Adjumani camp, we became convinced that God has brought us here. God has given us a world that cares. Whatever criticism that is leveled at the UNHCR, it is the organization that has helped us with material needs. Furthermore, even as I talk to you, a JRS person, I can tell you that I believe that JRS is one of the agencies sent by God to help us with spiritual and educational needs.

Don't misunderstand me. Life is not simple, and we all know the reality of an empty stomach; we all know the frustration of long lines and endless waiting. And so sometimes I am tempted to lose hope. But at such moments, I turn to prayer. Likewise, when there is sickness with me or with my family—and in the bush, as you know, there is much sickness—I pray, and often I am rescued either by a turn in the sickness or with caring medical people who see me and my family through the difficulty. In it all, I experience God's loving presence.

Cesaria, 41

I carry on this interview even though I am very sick: malaria. There have been lots of problems in my life, but I find God in my prayer and God gives me relief. I know God is with me. Let me give you an example. When we escaped from the war in Kajo Keji, we left with no food. Starving—we were starving. One night, we met a woman in the bush, a local in the area through which we were fleeing, and this woman gave us a goat so that we would not starve. Can you believe it? A goat! For me, it was a sign of God's care, and I never let my children forget it. They all remember when God sent an angel so that we would be properly fed. It kept us going until we arrived in Uganda.

And when we arrived in Uganda, there were hundreds, thousands of people waiting to be processed. It seemed like a hopeless wait, and then, in the midst of this huge crowd, we were called forward and we were registered right away and settled. Such a blessing.

When I think of God, when I say my prayers, I always remember how God protected me and my family as we ran from the killing of that terrible war.

Thomas, 32

My family is aware of God's presence. Both my wife and I came here at different times, but we both remember the escape, and I think it has influenced me ever since. I simply trust in God, and many times I have seen that trust show itself in the healing of my children when there was not time to get them to a doctor. Like getting out of the

Sudan, there are moments in sickness when you think you or your children will die, and yet you survive.

I think I am a catechist because I feel that since God has allowed me life, then it is important to share my life of God with others. My experience as a catechist has taught me that God is in my daily life and that God rewards our faithfulness. Sometimes I feel discouraged, but internally I am given strength—my vocation and my family somehow survive.

We struggle, particularly around food. But again, we trust in God, and somehow God, who brought us here and protected us on the way, will take care of us. My wife, too, is a sign of God in my everyday life. She helps me because of her love for me and because I can love her and the children.

Chaplain, 49

God kept me alive as we were escaping though the bush. We were fed by people along the way, and even when captured and beaten by the SPLA, the family managed to escape. [The SPLA] thought I was a government spy.

I have had many personal experiences of God's presence and care, above and beyond those moments of escape from the war. When I was a student at Maracha, at the school for catechists, my father appeared to me in a dream and told me that he was dying. The next day came and a messenger arrived with the news that my father, two days' travel away, was dying. I left immediately, and he died just after I arrived. I have always believed that God presents himself to us in a variety of ways, sometimes dramatically, like the protection of coming out of Sudan years ago, and sometimes this way, in a dream, making his love known by leading me to my father, whom I loved very much.

I become discouraged because, as you know, life is difficult, and there is no financial assistance given to the catechists even as they labor in the vineyard. I don't complain. I pray, and I do not lose hope, and God brings me back. I am called to be a catechist so that I can remind people that God does not forget his people.

My wife helps me find God every day, because I see her love for me and the children.

Paride, 43

There is a special image for me with regard to God and how God moves in my everyday experience of him. We were on the run and had been trapped by our pursuers. That image is one of sitting under a small tree with my child in my arms and bullets flying past us. I thought we were dead. We were not hit, and I realize every day that this was the moment in which God made himself present to me, and it is the moment upon which I always fall back when things are difficult.

I believe that I was spared to help others. And though I have been sick, though I was down with TB for a year, God has been present to lead me to recovery. I cannot leave the church because I am part of the church; to deny the Body of Christ would be to deny my experience of escape, and, as you can see, that experience has changed my life.

[My son] remembers that night of terror well, for his heart was beating up against mine. He knows God is with him.

Matilde, 49

I know that God is with us and that he comes with us daily in our life of work and sharing with others. God was with us in the suffering of the Sudan. He protected me and the family as we escaped.

I think I have suffered as much as anyone, especially in the loss of my children; some, as you know, were grown up and then died. God is aware of our suffering, and each day I commit myself to God and pray for the wisdom to get through and to be able to share in the suffering of others.

God makes himself, his love, known through the suffering of the refugees.

At every stage of their journey, whenever the cloud rose from the tabernacle the sons of Israel would resume their march. If the cloud did not rise, they waited and would not march until it did. For the cloud of Yahweh rested on the tabernacle by day, and a fire shone within the cloud by night, for all the House of Israel to see. And so it was for every stage of their journey. (Exodus 40:36–38)

A Love Story

I spent my first summer as a priest in a poor parish in San Diego.
One day I took communion to Cora and Wiley Gibson, an elderly couple
who lived near the church. When I arrived at their home, Cora greeted me
and led me into the living room, where her husband was sitting on the sofa.
He had no legs, long lost to the ravages of diabetes. He was blind and had
suffered a stroke that left one side of his face paralyzed. He couldn't talk and
could hear only if one shouted. Cora, a big and strong woman, assisted him
into a wheelchair and wheeled him outside to the porch, loudly announcing, "Wiley, Father is here to give you communion." He managed a crooked
smile and received the Host. She helped him masticate it.

As Cora and I gazed at Wiley, I thought, *This guy is blind, almost
deaf, partially paralyzed, and paraplegic. He's a mess.* Cora stood beside
me, her arms folded. She looked at Wiley, then at me, and then back to
him and said, "God, I love that man."

Her words crept over me and into me like the dawn. I understood
perhaps better than at any other time in my life the meaning of beauty.
The heart of God, wherein all beauty originates, sees not an ugly and
broken and insignificant man, but the interior beauty of the beloved.
And we are all beloved. Jesus emphasized the point by finding special
beauty in the least of our brothers and sisters.

Cora's piercing affection for Wiley was the beginning of my education in the power of love. The story of Moga and his wife, Rita, taught
me even more.

＊

Moga, a primary school supervisor on the JRS staff, called the JRS office in Adjumani from Zaipi, a town about fifteen miles away. He was with his wife, Rita, and she was dead. He asked if JRS could send a car to retrieve him, his father, his sister-in-law, and the body and take them home to their Ugandan village of Lefori. JRS quickly dispatched a car.

Moga is soft-spoken yet direct and has a quick, warm smile. A teacher in his late forties, he oversees several primary schools in the Adjumani network. He began working with JRS eleven years ago, following a long stint as the head teacher in a primary school in Kali, a small refugee village on the west side of the Nile, about twenty-five miles from the Sudan border. His wife, Rita, like Moga, had come to Uganda from Southern Sudan as a refugee in the nineties. She was forty-three when she died. They had been married for seventeen years, and they had five children, four boys and a girl, ranging in age from seven to fifteen.

Rita died from bilharzia, a water-borne disease common in the West Nile and Great Lakes regions. It is often contracted by bathing or swimming in water inhabited by snails that carry the parasitic worms. The parasite enters the human body through the skin, moves into the blood vessels, and lays eggs, which then travel to the intestines and the bladder and eventually on to the liver. If a person is exposed to a number of the parasites at once and the disease is not treated aggressively, it is merciless, causing a slow and painful death. Even after treatment, it may persist in the body. Symptoms of the disease include rash, fever, chills, muscle aches, coughing, liver swelling, and liver pain.

Rita had been treated in a hospital in Moyo, but the disease continued its advance. At the recommendation of the doctors, Moga packed Rita onto a bus and they made the 350-mile trip to Kampala, where there was better diagnostic equipment and more sophisticated treatment. While she was being treated in Kampala, she stayed with her sister. Moga returned to Adjumani and went to Kampala as often as he could.

Eventually, Rita's condition worsened, and she went into a coma. When Moga arrived, she was being fed by a tube and assisted mechanically in her breathing. What one of us, at a moment like this, would not want to take upon ourselves all the pain and discomfort and humiliation and bewilderment that our beloved is enduring? Who would not want to find some way, any way, to bring him or her a few minutes of painless peace?

Here was a man moving back and forth from the northern part of Uganda to Kampala, in the South, traveling on crowded clunker buses, spending much money on transportation, moving always in the tension of an army convoy that accompanies all buses because of potential ambushes by the LRA. And in all this, what was foremost in his mind was that the woman he loved, the mother of his children, was dying.

In Kampala, doctors told Moga that certain drugs would alleviate the crisis. Powerful antibiotics can be had if you have the money to purchase them. He moved around Kampala tracking the drugs and then spent half a million shillings (about $300—a person in his position may make anywhere from $100 to $200 per month) to obtain them. His thinking, he said, was *If I can get her communicating and sitting up, then I can bring her home.*

The drugs worked, and after three weeks Rita was able to talk. The catheters were removed and she was able to eat and take a few hesitant steps. Things were looking up, and Moga was feeling hopeful.

But then, perhaps ten days later, everything fell apart again, and Rita became violently ill. More drugs were prescribed. Wanting his wife to spend her last days at their home, Moga decided to take her out of the hospital. He persuaded the doctor to release her and bought bus tickets for himself, Rita, her sister, and his father, who had been helping Rita's sister look after her.

On the bus, Moga placed Rita, frail and dying, in the seat behind the driver, flanked by his father and her sister. The bus was so crowded, with everything from sweaty passengers to overstuffed luggage to live chickens, that Moga had to sit in the back.

It was Rita's last journey. Shortly before reaching Gulu, about seventy-five miles southeast of Adjumani, she died.

None of the other passengers knew she had died; she appeared as just another tired traveler, sleeping away the long trip. Moga decided to get off at the village of Zaipi, about sixty miles beyond Gulu and fifteen miles east of Adjumani. He wanted to avoid a large and nervous crowd that might materialize at the Adjumani bus park once people learned of the death.

This wasn't the end of Moga's long journey to get Rita home and give her a proper burial. He first had to purchase a coffin (Rita's parents insisted on this, instead of the typical burial in the ground with a cement covering). Father Pflueger, the JRS project director in Adjumani, offered financial assistance, and JRS staff raised additional money to help cover the funeral expenses. Finally, Rita was laid to rest.

After the funeral, I sat down with Moga to talk over the events of the past few days. One sees a lot of death and grief in the refugee camps, but sometimes there is so much that a man's response is stoic rather than emotional. But Moga's eyes filled with tears when I asked him what his concerns were now. His ordeal had been so unimaginably long and hard that his tears would have passed through granite in order that their truth might be claimed.

"The children," he whispered. "I am so worried about my children. They are without a mother now and often without me." He continued, stronger, but still in tears, "My parents are becoming old and weak; my father has had four hernia operations, and they cannot take care of these kids forever. I am far away and cannot always be there in case of sickness or a shortage of food and money. I am always moving."

I asked, "What kind of support do you have?"

"JRS has been good," he responded. "And God has given me power to keep going. I would not have been able to bring her back were it not for the help of God." It was beautifully expressed. His face said even more. God's love had sustained him and his hope and care for Rita. He was determined that this woman would end her trial with dignity and with her husband by her side. Nothing could have stopped him.

We sat for a moment in silence. Moga held his hand over his eyes.

I asked him then, "What is it about Rita that you most remember?"

He shook his head, raised his arm, and swept it around the room, a gesture we all use in the rush of poignant memories of those we cherish. He smiled and said, "You know, Father, she was always cooperative, industrious, hardworking, and loving. We never quarreled. She was a good mother to our children. In the end, she suffered a great deal but did so with courage. When she came out of her coma in the last session in Kampala, she was very happy because of my presence. To know I was there in all this misery meant a great deal for her—in one sense, everything. She was not alone because I was with her."

Like an individual faced with a long mountain climb, Moga marshaled his strengths, figured out what he had to do, renewed his commitment to his wife and to God, and then began the climb, from the first signs of illness to the final moments standing over Rita's grave. I never heard him complain, never saw him feel sorry for himself, and never knew him to waver from the course he had set.

"Rita always said in the final days in the Kampala hospital, 'Don't leave me here,'" Moga said.

He didn't.

Hakim

When Yahweh brought Zion's captives home,
at first it seemed like a dream;
then our mouths filled with laughter
and our lips with song.

—Psalm 126:1–2

Ezborn Hakim came to me after Sunday Mass at Agojo, a village of several thousand, a majority of whom are Catholics.
The village is famous for its polyphony of languages; I am told that between thirty-five and forty are spoken there. Hakim is the lead catechist of the Agojo chapel, and an outstanding one. He is admired by all his people, and his preaching is powerful, true, and unaffected. His warmth and affection for others emanates from his handshakes and embraces, his blazing smile and shining eyes. I benefit from not only his leadership in the church, but also his guidance, counsel, and inspired and clear understanding of Scripture.

After Mass, we chatted over tea. He asked if I would lend him the money to go to Southern Sudan, his home, to locate his older brother, whom he had learned was living in Juba. This would not be an ordinary visit, for he had not seen his brother in twenty years and, in fact, had assumed he was dead. During the war, Hakim's brother had become separated from the rest of the family. They had fled to Uganda, barely keeping ahead of Sudanese government soldiers. Two of Hakim's brothers and one of his sisters were killed in the escape. Eventually, those who made it safely to Uganda began to believe that everyone who had not made it had died. Now, it seemed that Hakim's brother was alive.

I gave Hakim about twenty dollars, enough to make the demanding five-day trip to Juba.

Weeks later, he came into the JRS office in Adjumani. He embraced me and repeatedly shook my hand. His happiness was irrepressible and contagious. Bubbling over with joy, his hands moving wildly about, he told me the story:

> I had been for twenty-two years without seeing my elder brother, Thomas Sebit. I discovered early this year that he was alive; for his part, he thought that I and the family had perished in the course of time or had been killed on the night we all fled from the soldiers.
>
> I left on the twelfth of June, and by foot, bike, bus, and taxi, I reached Juba on the sixteenth. . . . From the outskirts of Juba, I proceeded to that part of the city where my informant had told me my brother lived. As I approached the area, I met a woman who was selling her mugati [bread]. When I asked about my brother, she said—I could not believe it, sincerely— "Yes, I know him; he has just passed by here."
>
> I asked, "Could you please go and look for him?"
>
> She said, "Yes, I can."
>
> She left and swiftly found my Thomas. I found out later that when she told him that his younger brother Hakim was there looking for him, he could not agree with her and was angry. "Do not joke with me," he said. "My brother Hakim is dead."

She said, "Come and see." And he came.

I was waiting on the road when I saw them walking toward me with many others who had also heard through the woman that I had come to see my brother. My brother was well-known in this part of Juba because he is a headmaster of a local school.

When seeing me, he started running toward me and crying, and then I started to cry, and we embraced and fell to the ground crying. We just held on to each other for thirty minutes and cried. You must understand that we both thought that the other had died. Brothers! Still brothers! We were surrounded by many people all rejoicing with us. Eventually my brother said, "Let us go home."

So we set off for his home, and on the way we met with his wife. Her name is Mary. And telling his wife, "This is my brother, whom we thought was dead," she also began to cry. When we reached home, a number of people came to see me, and seeing me, who Thomas had said had died, they could not agree, since it was clear we looked like each other. Everyone was crying. And then we started laughing. We were laughing and crying at the same time.

And here was an amazing thing: Thomas said that they had organized my last funeral rite in April of this year, around the time I had heard he was still alive. He had done this because they had learned that many people had been killed or sentenced to death in Uganda and I was one of them. I answered him that I am alive over all these years, but he was not agreeing even as he was agreeing.

So he kept me in the house for three days to make sure I wasn't a ghost. And we talked and talked and wept and wept. After three days my brother agreed that it was me, and many people came to see me, and we all shared in the joy of the occasion by slaughtering a goat and eating it with many other nice things.

I stayed with my brother for two weeks.

On my way back to the Adjumani settlement and my village of Agojo, I kept thinking of and praying about a passage from the Gospel of John, and especially John 16:16, 20–22:

"In a short time you will no longer see me,
and then a short time later you will see me again.". . .

"I tell you most solemnly,
you will be weeping and wailing
while the world will rejoice;
you will be sorrowful,
but your sorrow will turn to joy.
A woman in childbirth suffers,
because her time has come;
but when she has given birth to the child she forgets
    the suffering
in her joy that a man has been born into the world.
So it is with you: you are sad now,
but I shall see you again, and your hearts will be full
    of joy,
and that joy no one shall take from you."

※

What is really important in this life? Not the acquisition of material things, because they are never enough for our human hunger; not reputation, because someone always comes along who is smarter and cleverer; not beauty, because that fades and there will always be someone more beautiful. For me, it always comes down to human connection, to relationship, to being loved and giving in love. Amid so much death—from disease, from war, from the convulsions of a difficult life—life is renewed in human connection. This is brought home for me every time I witness a reunion like the one between Hakim and his brother. Our greatest gift in life is the love for and of others, which is born of God's love for us.

A Bridge to the Eternal

Adjumani, 1:30 a.m. The call came half an hour ago: Andy Dufner is dead. After hanging up, I smiled at the thought that Dufner, a scientist, would have been fascinated by how fast word could travel between Portland and northern Uganda. Then I wept. A line from Bob Dylan's "I'll Remember You" kept bouncing around in my head:

> In the end, my dear sweet friend, I'll remember you.

Although he was back home in Oregon, Dufner was with me in Africa every day: in his friendship, in his encouragement, in his prayer. He was the one who helped me sort through my instincts about Africa and helped me throughout my long process of discernment. Once I was in Uganda, he was the one I called when I needed to talk. He was the first person I went to when I had a rare break in the States.

Another's love holds us close, accompanies us, challenges us, influences our choices and perspectives and worldview, leads us to open doors and directs us away from dead ends. So it was with Andy's love for me. Much of what I have come to understand about my heart and myself in Africa I arrived at through his constant support and belief in me. For decades, this good man shared in all my major sorrows and triumphs. I grew in sharing my life with him, as a tree grows with help from the sun.

☀

When I was home in the States for a break three weeks ago, I visited Dufner. Coming from a place where I see death and near death every day, I now faced the reality of one of my best friends battling cancer. Dufner looked gaunt, but he was full of love and wisdom and laughter. His attitude was encouraging.

He had the interior life of a saint and the brain of a scientist (with a PhD in high-speed particle physics), making him a unique patient who understood better than most the high stakes of colon cancer and the language of oncologists and the consequences of aggressive chemotherapy.

It was important for me to be with him. He had been with me in my joy and my despair, in howling successes and near meltdowns. I loved him deeply. We never finished a conversation on the phone over my five years in Africa without telling each other, "I love you." When he was in Portland for chemotherapy, we often had early-morning coffee together. Of course, we talked of death; he was ready for whatever God would give him—and joyfully transparent in his readiness.

Now I stand naked before this death. I keep commending all my tears and grief to God, knowing that, in the end, Dufner was a gift to me from God. When I last held Dufner in my arms, on a crispy fall day in Portland shortly before I returned to Adjumani, we both knew that it would probably be the last time we would see each other in this life. I flashed on the words of Raymond Carver, writing after his diagnosis of terminal cancer, in "Proposal":

> Back home we held on to each other and, without
> embarrassment or caginess, let it all reach full
>   meaning. This
> was it, so holding back had to be stupid, had to be
> insane and meager. How many ever get to this?

Now Dufner is dead and knows face-to-face our eternal loving God, whose creation he, as a physicist, spent his life explaining and whose heart he, as a lover, spent his life extolling.

The Rings of the Sitka Spruce

Dufner and I met in Oakland in the seventies. I was a hotshot community organizer, on a leave of absence from the Jesuits and badly in need of spiritual direction. He was on the board of directors of the fledgling organizing project in impoverished East Oakland for which I worked.

That leave of absence lasted seven years. Probably once a month as I worked through it, I would see him for spiritual guidance in Berkeley, where he worked in administration at the Jesuit School of Theology. There I would uncover as much of my soul as I could and ramble through my latest crisis. I was full of anger in those days, taking most of it out on slumlords and an out-of-touch Oakland government. Dealing with me was like handling a pile of burning charcoal, but Dufner could do it.

We kept in touch even after those days in Oakland. One snowy night, from a phone booth in Toronto, I called him at Seattle University, where he was teaching. I was approaching the decision to finally leave or stay with the Jesuits and the priesthood. He said, "Follow your heart, Smith. It's a good heart. Know that I love you." Over the years he was my mentor, my spiritual director, my brother, and my friend—my main man. His friendship is one of the finest things I can say of myself.

Little things about him come to mind. For example, he used to explain things to me scientifically with this towering patience, as if he really believed I could understand. Once, as he was microwaving his strange breakfast gruel—a combination of grains, water, fruit, and one "mystery element" that changed each day—I asked him how microblasting the elements produced the end result, and he answered over his shoulder, "It is a function of atmospheric pressure and humidity." Simple. I gave him my best gimlet-eyed stare and said, like I had countless times before and after, "I don't know what the hell you're talking about." We'd laugh, and then it was off to breakfast, where he'd eat his risky, awful-looking mush and I'd eat my safe, attractive Raisin Bran and we'd talk as the sun came up. I couldn't say how many times the two of us sat at that table and had our crack-of-dawn heart-to-heart summit conferences.

Like all individuals who open their hearts, he remained in me and in others whatever the separations of time and distance. There is this giant Sitka spruce that benevolently dominates part of the road that leads into the Nestucca Sanctuary, the Jesuit retreat facility on the Oregon coast that he founded and ran. I used to ask him, "How old do you think that tree is, Dufner?" He would eyeball it and give the scientific Dufnerian answer, "About five hundred years." "Nope," I'd say, "you're wrong; it's at least a million." We'd have a good laugh. Either way you calculated, it was an oldie and a goody—massive, craggy, and the undisputable elder of the sanctuary's tree world. What mysterious moments of forest life over the centuries would that tree disclose if we looked carefully at its rings? Those of us who knew and loved Dufner can look at the interior of the tree that is our life and discover rings that have his name on them. In our growing process, he was there.

The Heart of Nestucca and the Heart of Christ

Nestucca Sanctuary was a dream Dufner realized with a handful of others. It was lived and developed in large part with Colleen, his assistant, and the two of them mastered the art of hospitality. This simple retreat house in the forest has attracted thousands over nearly two decades. Down that approach road come individuals beaten by life and running on empty, as well as those overflowing with self-confidence, and every sort of individual in between. Nestucca offers a space where all can take themselves into their arms and be taken into those of others.

Many come: students, the homeless, lawyers, the physically and mentally challenged, gray-bearded Jesuits and Jesuit novices, business-people, contractors, ministers of all faiths, vagabonds, college professors, religious women and men from many communities, poets, artists, peace and justice activists, physicians, veterans, and women who feel alienated by the church. Dufner had a special place in his heart for the poor and those who work with the poor. Nestucca attracts people who are easy with the institutional church and those who are gagging on doctrine and dogma, but there is a common tenderness among Nestucca guests, even among the most wounded and cynical. The place can unleash that quality of the heart.

People can find what they need there while respecting the needs of each other. If you want total quiet, you can have it; if you want community, it is there. If you want to sort stuff out, if you want to discover the God of the stars and the rivers, Nestucca is the place to do so.

At the center of the day is the Eucharist, offered simply and profoundly. The moments of bread breaking around the table in front of the fireplace draw participants into a mystery that reflects the sacred heart of Nestucca, and—as Dufner would say—that heart is the loving heart of Christ enhancing and uniting us all.

It is a holy place.

Dufner never kidded himself about the driving force behind the holiness. He knew he was only an instrument of the holy, no doubt a most talented one, and every nail he pounded and every piece of plumbing he installed and every new energy conservation system he mounted and every annoying bump on the road he removed with his little Kubota tractor—all these things were part of that holiness.

This Nestucca holiness was incarnated especially in the hours and hours he spent with people, accepting them unconditionally and believing in their intrinsic ability to grow and claim their lives before God. I think he was especially alert and sensitive to those who arrived marching to the beat of a different drum. He was a man for all seasons and for all people, a loving guy. Although he was an introvert, he always opened his heart for those who sought him out. Some visitors were holy; many were dealing with the million conflicts and questions that attend the human condition. But we were all people who needed someone to help us understand the power of the Spirit that was compelling our hearts, our lives, and our vision. He was that person.

That so many different individuals come to Nestucca is a testimony to its vision. On certain nights, as I looked at those assembled around the dinner table, an image would come to mind of the *Star Wars* bar where weirdos from every part of the universe gathered for a drink and a little "So what's going on in your galaxy?" conversation. We were all human beings, but with such diversity.

Around that table we would eat delicious food and engage in enlightening dialogues. And laugh. We laughed a lot. After all that wonderful food, out would come the ice cream, cheapo stuff that Dufner liked. I used to sanctimoniously say that artificially flavored ice cream was unhealthy. His response: "Scientific proof, Smith?" Me: "I don't have any data." Laughter. Me again: "Uh, could you please pass the Chunky Chocolate?"

A Bridge to the Ocean

We'd sit at that table, Dufner and I, sometimes by ourselves and sometimes with others, looking at the Pacific Ocean through the big lodge windows and musing about a method of crossing the Nestucca River to the small spit of land, perhaps two hundred yards out, that separated the river from the ocean—a method of crossing that would eliminate the twenty-five minute drive to the ocean. We had lots of goofy ideas. His were from a scientific perspective, so they were probably better. My ideas were naive and dumb, although I always tried to be ecologically correct, a quality that caused Dufner to pause for a moment in appreciation before dismantling them. There were legendary beauties: a giant slingshot (negative: might ruin the trees, although the idea of placing a huge pillow on the other side intrigued him); an under-the-river tube (negative: might disturb the ecosystem of the river); and a submarine that I saw sitting in the Willamette River in Portland. And so we went. Honest to God, we used to entertain ourselves for hours—for years.

But there is a deeper point: the perfect river crossing was a metaphor for our connection, Andy with me and me with Andy. And we never had to figure it out. The two of us could always build a bridge to each other instantly, spontaneously, whether we were together or communicating from thousands of miles away. It could be built in silence, in a knowing glance across the room, or in a two-hour conversation. No goofy ideas about the nature of this relationship. The connection to the ocean of each other's heart was real, solid, direct, and steadfast. That connection now exists in an eternal arena.

Holy Week and a Cloud of Witnesses

Holy Thursday

I celebrated Holy Thursday Mass at Okusijoni, where most of the Catholics are Acholi. In spite of its proximity to the Nile, the area is very dry, parched and uninviting. Standing in stark contrast to the barren landscape was the small army of children who welcomed me as I drove up to the chapel.

Juma Santo, the catechist, and I discussed the liturgy, and then he departed to change clothes, since he had been planting maize on my arrival. I was left in the thatched chapel with probably fifty grinning, wide-eyed four- to six-year-olds seated on the log pews. One of the children in the front row, a girl missing her two front teeth, started singing, and instantly the chapel was transformed into a concert hall, filled with children warbling like birds at dawn. They sang everything they knew. And then sang it again. They couldn't understand a word of English but were watching my face to determine if I was enjoying their songs. I thanked them in Acholi, which made them happy. Then I pulled out my puppet Scovia, and *she* thanked them in Acholi. They went nuts.

At one point in the liturgy, I knelt on the dirt floor of the chapel and washed the feet of several elderly people, including a widow of seventy, Lillian Okaya. In the settlements, shoes are rare, and socks nonexistent. The feet of those poor people who work their meager plots of land are, like their hands, worn, leathery, and dirty. After I finished washing the twelve selected for the occasion, Lillian washed my smooth and absurdly clean feet. I looked down at her; over my years here, she has come to consider me as her son. She raised and lost six children, three by disease and three in the Sudan civil war, along with her husband. It was a humbling moment.

For me, Jesus' act of carefully washing the feet of his disciples, as a slave would wash the feet of his owner, contains the biggest mystery of all. I know that I circle Christ's love in this ritual, eventually submitting to the centripetal force of that love. I understand that love, but I don't understand it. I get it, but I don't get it. As I washed the feet of the Okusijoni people and they mine, I looked into their faces of faith. They get it.

At the end of the Mass, I asked Susan, one of the women leaders in the chapel, to offer a closing prayer. She is twenty-five, the mother of four, and possesses a smile that could light up the darkest night. She prayed, her eyes closed, holding her six-month-old baby in her arms, the child's head resting tranquilly on Susan's shoulder. She rocked slightly as she prayed. The chapel was hushed; even the noises of the bush seemed muted. Juma told me after Mass that she prayed for a deeper understanding of the humility of God. And she prayed for me, that I would be protected from all dangers, from discouragement, and from sickness, and that I would know the gratitude of the people of Okusijoni for sharing my faith with them. Now isn't that the ironic clincher? Me sharing my faith with them? Isn't it *they* who are sharing their faith with *me*?

Good Friday

Frido, the director of the JRS project in Adjumani, joined me today at the village of Kobo for the Good Friday liturgy. Every year he comes with me on Good Friday.

The Kobo "chapel" is on a small promontory that overlooks the West Nile. Large rocks beneath a towering tree on the promontory serve as pews.

I always come to chapels in the villages mentally prepared for snafus, big and small. Sure enough, today the catechist, Simon, forgot to bring a cross—*on Good Friday*. And, too, the poor man was the only one present who could read, let alone read in Bari, the language of the people, so he wound up reading John's entire Passion account as well as the intercessions of the Good Friday liturgy. It was a lot of words and he was agonizingly slow, but it didn't bother the people, who listened intently. Simon is a simple man, liked by all.

Soon it was time for the veneration of the cross. What to do about the crucifix? Fortunately, I had with me an ebony cross about fifteen inches high, one with a corpus. But the corpus had broken loose from the cross during the trip to Kobo. I took a rubber band I found stashed in my backpack and used it to bind Jesus around his chest to the cross. Then we had to figure out how to prop up the crucifix during veneration. Frido suggested banding the cross and corpus to his aluminum water container, which was originally a bottle of Danish vodka. Once assembled, we placed the crucifix in all its black beauty on the little altar.

The veneration by the congregation was direct, their faith bringing new meaning to liturgical propriety. The people of Kobo—first the elders, then the younger people, and finally the children—approached the crucifix and, kneeling reverently on a papyrus mat, bowed before the cross, or kissed the feet of the corpus, or reached out just to touch. It was an unfettered and tender piety. How could it be otherwise? Sudanese refugees know better than most the cold blade of physical and emotional suffering; they know the cruelty of injustice; and they know the size and power of sacrificial love rendered for the beloved.

After we had made our own veneration, Frido and I stood off to the side and watched the people come to the crucifix, bound with a rubber band to a vodka bottle. I whispered to him, "Can we possibly forget this Good Friday?" He shook his head. "Never."

Easter Vigil

This afternoon I was at Oliji, a village of Madi-speaking Catholics next to the Nile led by a well-organized young catechist named Andruga. The liturgy was under a tree again, since part of the chapel roof burned down when leaders tried to smoke out a colony of termites.

A large and enthusiastic crowd—maybe three hundred people—greeted me as I pulled in to the village an hour before Mass. I heard confessions, not understanding much but able to absolve in Madi. Midway through the confessions, which took place under the chapel tree, a powerful thunderstorm blew through, forcing us to continue under a section of the chapel roof that was still intact.

Because of security issues on the roads after dark, I needed to start the vigil at 4:00 p.m., which took the punch out of the Service of Light. But adjustment is easy for people who adjust all the time. There were thirty-one baptisms. By the time I was through anointing all the little heads and chests, three-quarters of the babies were screaming. The people loved it, though, and at the conclusion of the ceremony everyone applauded and the women ululated and the choir unleashed some wonderful music. Like a speeding locomotive, we blazed into the Easter "Gloria."

After Mass, Andruga and I, with many of the women, walked to the edge of the village to visit a sick woman named Lucietta. Andruga wanted me to anoint her and give her communion. The women assisted her out of her hut to a mat underneath a tree, formed a circle around her, and sang and prayed: Oliji's cloud of witnesses. Lucietta probably weighed about eighty pounds, and in her serene and welcoming face I could detect a hint of a Parkinson's-like tremor. She looked old but did not know her age. She remained silent throughout the ceremony, a ritual with which she was familiar, having many times before been part of the circle.

After the women finished, I knelt in front of Lucietta and anointed her hands and head, then gave her communion. I carefully took her beautiful, tremulous face in my hands, tilting her head so that she could look into my eyes, and blessed her. In such a moment, when the near-death anointed one looks at me, everything I have ever studied about sacraments of encounter becomes clear. I rested silently before an obvious and splendid truth: this touch was an encounter with the heart of God.

She asked me in Madi, "What is your name?"

I responded in Madi, "My name is Gary, Abuna Gary."

She peered into my face, smiled, and exclaimed, "This is a Madi name!" (There is a Madi word, *gaari*, that means "bicycle.") Then she slowly said, "Abuna Gaari" and laughed. I laughed. The cloud of witnesses laughed.

We left her sitting prayerfully on her mat and headed for the pickup—Andruga, those wonderful women, and me, Father Bicycle. Later, driving on the bumpy road toward Adjumani, dusk settling in, I commented to Ratib that if I was going to fight for God, all I wanted backing me up were the women of Oliji, armed with the most powerful of weapons: their prayer. Ratib, a Madi and a Muslim, nodded reflectively and said, "A good choice, Father, a good choice."

Easter Sunday

This morning, as I headed for the village of Dubaju, I encountered soldiers stationed in pickups on one of the three dirt roads that lead in and out of Adjumani. A district special election is to be held next week, and they were there in anticipation of possible violence. I was a bit unnerved by their guns and frowning faces. But my anxiety was dispelled when, about a hundred meters from the Dubaju chapel, I was greeted by twenty dancing children. Preceding my pickup in two lines, they led me to the chapel area, singing and dancing and clapping all the way.

I was tired, but I was energized during Mass by a happy, excited group of worshipers singing in several African languages. After Mass, delegated members of the congregation gave Easter speeches while I sat down and relaxed. At one point, a little girl, Kiden, maybe three years old, came up to my chair, crawled into my lap, and fell asleep. Apparently, Kiden and some buddies had recently made a raid on a mango tree, so she was covered in mango juice, which meant that half of the flies in the Nile valley were drawn to her, a fact of which she was blissfully unaware. Eventually, as the Easter talks were ending, her grandmother appeared, hoisted the sleepyhead from my lap, and then disappeared with her into the crowd.

I think of Kiden in my arms: isn't this a metaphor for the JRS mandate to accompany the refugees of the world? Kiden's little life is besieged constantly by deprivation and exploitation, yet in my arms—beating heart against beating heart—she could experience her dignity, that promised and sanctified human dignity that is at the shining center of Christ's resurrection.

A Long Night's Journey into Day

They went away, went away weeping,
carrying the seed;
they come back, come back singing,
carrying their sheaves.

—Psalm 126:6

The peace treaty between the government of Sudan and the Sudan People's Liberation Army ends a long night's journey for the tens of thousands of Sudanese refugees in Uganda. The dawn of peace allows them to survey the returning road ahead. As Americans have their Civil War battleground names as part of their historical consciousness, so the Sudanese have theirs: Kajo Keji, Juba, Yei, Bahr el-Ghazal, Nimule, Wau, Yambio, Torit, Khartoum, Arua, Moyo, Koboko, Rhino Camp, Adjumani, Invepi, Palorinya. The road they have traveled is strewn with fear and grief and the heartache of senseless killing. On the other hand, the journey has toughened their hearts, as their work on the land has calloused their hands. Those hearts are full of determination, faith, and abiding hope.

After a Mass in Obilokongo, I was sitting with several leaders, having tea and talking about our families. The conversation turned to children and how many children each person had lost. No one had lost less than two. Taban said, "I had eleven children; four remain." "And the other seven?" I asked. "Three have died of disease, and four were shot when we were fleeing Sudan. They were killed in front of me. Even after peace, I shall return on paths full of bad memories."

"They came in the night," said Archangelo as we walked along a bush road paralleling the Nile near his village of Oliji. "I was seven. We piled onto a lorry heading south, and it was hit by a grenade and knocked off the road. Everyone fled. My family and I were separated, and I never saw them again. I was eventually handed over to UNHCR and taken to Kenya, then to the Congo, and now I am here in Uganda, trying to finish secondary school. I ask God each day to lead me and prepare me for my life in Sudan."

Refugees speak of the return journey. They will carry with them a lot of baggage: for those who fled, memories of home, of tragedy, of bitterness toward their enemies, of depending on handouts, of being strangers in Uganda. For the children born in Uganda, it will be a journey into the unknown, into places and faces they have only heard of in conversations or seen in the weeping eyes of their elders. What will be different for the young is that this new home will be a permanent home.

"Yes, we will go back," said Kenyi, the bright young leader and catechist in Kali, in the Palorinya settlement. "I came when I was fourteen; now I am twenty-nine. Already some of our family has gone ahead to begin building and planting. We will do the same with the church. Next year, Abuna, you will be invited to visit us and offer Mass for us."

Latiku is from the village of Ibibiaworo, which overlooks the Nile valley. "I came to the Adjumani Refugee Settlement ten years ago. There were many tribes. For example, in Agojo, there are over thirty languages spoken. But people, in spite of tribal differences, lived peacefully together most of the time; we have been through too much to fight among ourselves in these circumstances. There has to be unity—as best as we can build it—if we are going to build a new Sudan."

The return is complicated. Many factors inhibit a swift return. For example, while the Sudanese in the South will no longer be subject to the oppressive administration of the Sudan government, they have concerns about the style of democracy instituted by the SPLA. They take a wait-and-see attitude, even though I sense that they see autocracy with one's own people as better than an endless war with the North.

A Sudanese NGO staffer working in Southern Sudan, reflecting over a beer, related this story: "This young kid got drunk and came to a local bar around Christmas and shot an adversary. Killed him. The shooter was sixteen. The SPLA arrested him and three days later executed him by firing squad. The whole town was told to come and witness the punishment. The SPLA will not allow anyone to get out of control. They have invested too much in this fight. Law and order will prevail. Certainly order. These guys will be running the new Sudan."

Another question mark in the minds of some refugees is what to do about personal and professional investments. In Adjumani, for example, many men have businesses that they will not abandon, meaning that the mother and children will return alone. And because of the instability of the education system in Sudan, secondary students may remain in Uganda for a while. This is not the case in the lower grades. Already numbers are dropping in JRS nursery and primary schools in northern Uganda. Another factor is the question of repatriation by the UNHCR. Some will wait for the UNHCR to provide transportation, rations, cookware, blankets, and other items for the trip home.

"Are you going soon?" I asked a woman of Dongo, in the Palorinya settlement. "Well, much of this depends on the UNHCR," she answered. "We will go when we have something to go with. The drought may eliminate any food we could take with us, so we will depend on them to help. . . . For many of us, there are no resources to move."

Naturally, peace brings happiness and joy. And yet, amid the dancing, an ominous dark cloud continues to hang over the North, which everyone watches cautiously: the conflict in the region of Darfur, in which it is estimated that nearly four hundred thousand have been killed, and two million displaced, as the Sudanese military and militia groups fight against various rebel groups. Here one sees the Khartoum tactics that were once visited upon the South. This intensifies the doubt and suspicion that some have regarding the peace treaty: they know that there have been double-crosses in the past. There exists within the refugee community a lingering distrust—they remember the fight and the danger of the fight; nevertheless, it does not trump their hope or stall the short-term and long-term preparations for the journey back to Sudan.

"Do you think the peace will hold?" I asked an Adjumani refugee leader. He replied, "I think so." Then he added, a tense smile on his face, "But we will be watchful. I never trust the Arabs."

Recently, the Lord's Resistance Army made incursions into the Adjumani villages on the eastern fringe of the settlement, forcing many of our people to leave their villages and JRS to close several nursery, primary, and secondary schools and abandon pastoral work in about ten chapels. For days, the roads heading into Adjumani were filled with people carrying possessions on their heads and babies on their backs and leading their goats and other animals by ropes.

This scene was for me a metaphor for the larger picture of the refugee's life: always on the move. But for thousands, this latest attack prompted them to continue north: past Adjumani, across the Nile, through Moyo, and back to Sudan. Back home, to the promise of a new day. The hope I hear is that this will be the last night of a journey born of the insanity of war. Whatever lingering doubts, almost everyone now talks of going home, of following those who have fled the LRA killing machine and finding the long-denied light and peace.

Say Yes Again and Forgive Forever

The meeting of the four catechist zone leaders of the Palorinya Refugee Settlement took place at Belameling, deep in the settlement and adjacent to the Nile. The catechist zone leader is responsible for as many as five villages within the settlement, planning training sessions for catechists and the chapel congregations, observing chapel catechists at work, and coordinating with JRS on behalf of the chapels to obtain needed items, such as liturgical books in native languages, Bibles, and teaching materials.

This particular meeting was held to plan programs for the next several months. The four zone leaders—Wurube, Osura, Dima, and Eiyo—came from the four corners of the settlement and represented twenty-one chapels. These four are some of the best catechists I have worked with in my two years in Adjumani.

After an excellent exchange of ideas and tea and a few biscuits, Osura's wife, Julieta, joined our little circle. A Madi by tribe, Julieta is a tall woman with a strikingly long jaw and small eyes set deep in her face. She has given birth to eight children, six of whom are still alive. She was wearing an orange dress and a brilliant red headscarf. Her neck, typical of most African women who carry loads on their heads, was long and muscled, yet delicate.

Wurube, the lead catechist for the entire settlement, informed me that Julieta wanted to address me and the others. I wondered what she could possibly want to talk about. I knew that she had been sick, so perhaps she was going to request money for medicine with the support of the other catechists.

But I was wrong.

As she began to talk, she made no eye contact with any of us in the room. Off to her left, sitting on another log bench, was Osura. What followed was an event I had never before experienced in the African culture: a complaint by a wife of her husband in front of a group of elders—in this case, the three other catechist leaders and myself. By addressing us with her complaint, she invested us with the responsibility usually reserved for village elders; by listening, we accepted our role.

Julieta's words came out hard and fast, like a river pouring out of her heart. Her face reflected many feelings: sadness, anger, frustration, and determination. Dima translated for me:

"I am bewildered. My husband is a drunkard. He not only drinks, but when he drinks he comes home to engage in petty arguments with me and then finishes off his disagreement with me by abusing me verbally and physically, hitting me in the face and on my ribs. One night in an argument, he hit me with a half-full water can and then poured the water on my mattress. We disagreed so much that now, to my embarrassment, and before the entire community, he has moved from our home and lives in the small house near the church, and I suspect he is in a compromising situation with one particular woman. I am not sure of what is going on, but I have my suspicions."

Osura was looking off into space, his foot jittery and bouncing, his lips pressed together tightly. My heart was sinking in this naked disclosure about one of my best catechists and his wife.

Julieta continued, her lips quivering, her extended finger angrily poking holes in the air: "I have been so tormented about all this that I have not set foot in this chapel for over a year. For over a year. He says all these nice things in the chapel, but at home he acts the opposite. It is hypocritical, and I am very angry about it. How can he preach about the love of God and then go out and drink and argue with me, hit me? And not only me, but many others. It is no secret that he does this, all of which makes me wonder who he is. This is not the man I married."

There was silence. I was astonished by this moment of brutal honesty. Wurube then asked Osura if he would like to respond. Osura is a six-foot-tall, big-boned man with a broad face and huge eyes that light up when he is teaching. Those eyes dart and flash in moments of anger, as they were now. Until that moment, I had only seen that anger when he was attacking an injustice. He is fluent in several languages, but he spoke Bari now.

He was embarrassed that his family troubles were being aired before his colleagues and me. On the other hand, he accepted that he must respond, given that elders were present. He was translated for me by Wurube:

"Julieta knows that I married her many years ago because I wanted to. I came asking for her; she did not come asking for me. I sought her out, and ten years ago we were married in this chapel in the full sacramental expression of our love. And God has blessed us with several children. We loved each other. But she came from a clan that saw evil spirits everywhere—in the creation, in all people, and ultimately in me. And she could become a witch in this family if she wanted to. But she agreed to give all this up when she married me, yet now it looks like all this is coming back again, and she sees evil spirits everywhere and is acting like a witch toward me."

Osura paused; his foot had stopped moving.

"A lot of my drinking is caused by my confrontation with her beliefs in these matters, but I do not drink that much, and I have never been drunk; and when I struck her—once or twice—I did it with an open hand."

Julieta was shaking her head fiercely in denial.

Osura continued: "Yes, I moved out, because I could not take the constant argument. There is no happy face that greets me when I come home, but the face of anger and words that attack me. The water incident is not true, and it was an accident that water was poured on her mattress. But we are so unhappy that it is impossible for me to remain under the same roof, so I moved down here to the small house connected with the chapel. The other woman implication is not true."

Again there was silence. I was not sure what the custom was, but I instinctively felt that everyone was expecting the priest to respond first. I was right. Wurube turned to me and asked my opinion. I addressed Osura, with Dima translating:

"Osura, your words say one thing, and your face and wife say another. I think you are in denial of how serious things are around the drinking. You must look with a wise eye at the drinking, because this seems to be where the trouble begins. Furthermore, there is no excuse for you to hit your wife, or any woman. Ever. Look at yourself: you are big, tall, strong, intimidating. Even I, taller than you, would be overmatched. Let there be tranquillity on the waters of your marriage. If the liquor in any way is a cause of trouble, then stop drinking. Let this marriage be cleared of the darkness that I see on your face and Julieta's."

Wurube thanked me and then asked Eiyo for her comments. She is a longtime religious leader in her community and walked for two hours to get to this meeting. She has given birth to eleven children in her forty-five years, six of whom have died. Her husband is also dead, killed in the Sudanese civil war. For all her suffering as a single mother, she is an extraordinarily handsome and young-looking woman. She turned to Osura and addressed his drinking:

"Osura, you must stop the drinking, not just for your marriage's sake, but because everyone in your chapel knows about it and whispers behind your back: 'Oh, he says one thing but does the other.' In the end, your community will not respect your words. And, therefore, they will not respect you. This is bad, because you are to be an example to your people. I know the people of this chapel, so I do not speak with ignorance or as a woman blindly supporting a sister. And now that you are choosing to be separated from your wife, what kind of statement is that to the couples in your chapel, most of whom struggle with the question of proper marriage? These events have not remained in your zone and in this chapel. Many of us have heard rumors."

Eiyo's words were a direct hit. Everyone was somber. I was holding my breath. I have known Eiyo for five years. She is a truth teller and takes no nonsense from anyone. I had never seen her more powerful and direct.

Dima spoke next. He is an intelligent man in his mid-forties, married and the father of five. His eldest son, at seventeen, died suddenly last year of cerebral malaria. Dima has movie-star looks and always speaks calmly and commands attention because he never wastes words.

He addressed Osura:

"Osura, for years we have been together as brothers, trying to keep our faith safe among our people in spite of war and disruption and sickness and death. . . . And so, as a brother united to you over all these years, I have to tell you that there is no way you could ever justify striking your wife. She is a human being and deserves respect, no matter what your disagreement with each other is. How are we to strengthen our women's rights in our culture if *catechists* are striking their wives? How is any woman in your chapel going to listen to you when they know that you have hit their sister? How can we say that we follow the peaceful and loving Jesus when we are attacking our own wives? How can your children, especially your daughters, know you in any other way than in fear if they see their mother, who carried them in her womb, beaten by their own father? Will they not say, 'Are we next?' And will your sons drink this poison that seems to justify abuse of a woman? My brother, stop this now."

He turned to Julieta: "And Julieta, my sister, you must now begin to greet Osura with a cheerful face when he comes into your home. You must welcome your husband and forgive as he must forgive and change his ways and his attitude."

At this point, I felt tears coming down my face. I was moved by the powerful, compassionate, and penetrating candor of Eiyo and Dima. The pain of Julieta and Osura's past and the leaders' utter honesty seized me, coalesced in me, and brought to the surface all my empathy and longing for wholeness for such wonderful and wounded people. And, too, memories were unleashed in me, storms moving across my interior terrain: I have known alcoholism in my own family, and I have seen the children of alcoholism on the streets of the United States—I know its method of madness involves denial and lashing out at the one who exposes the painful truth.

Wurube then spoke. As the lead catechist of the settlement, chosen by all the catechists to unite them and speak for them, he is the local refugee contact person for the archdiocese and the nearest Ugandan priest. He is in his forties and is married to one of the sweetest and kindest women God has ever created, Mary. They have five girls, who smother me with hugs when I come to their poor compound. Wurube is wiry and full of energy. He is a good teacher and listener and can capture any audience with his contagious enthusiasm for his subject matter. Like Dima and Eiyo, he is respected by the catechists across Palorinya.

He said: "My sister and brother, you both are blessed by God to have the courage to speak this way to us and to invite our opinion. There must now be a renewal of your commitment to each other. You must now say yes again to each other and forgive forever. Let all this anger and drinking and abuse and hostility and separation stop. You must turn to God in this, even as you must turn to each other in honesty and seek to find the love that you first had, that produced your wonderful children, a sign of God's love for his world.

"Julieta, return to church; support your husband. Let him see all his people when he leads them in prayer and there especially let him see his wife, who believes in him and his words. Osura, you must forgive and ask forgiveness and stop those actions that have caused so much heartache in your wife. Look at her face; it is the face of suffering and the face of longing to love and be with her husband of old. Let your children know happiness once again in a family where they deserve happiness and laughter."

When Wurube concluded his counsel, we had been at it for well over an hour. I was drenched in sweat from the intensity of the sharing, helped by the extreme heat of the afternoon.

Then Osura spoke, thanking us all for entering with love into their personal problems. His big eyes were tearful, but clear. He asked his wife's forgiveness and told her that he would seek to correct the things that had precipitated the crisis. All nodded, even Julieta, who, for the first time, was looking at her husband, discerning his words, his gestures. There was peace on her face. It had been a long journey for her, and this sharing had been such a colossal risk. But she knew that if she brought her complaint before the elders, they would be bound to respond, and Osura would be bound to listen and respond as well. I had been taken into a most amazing world.

Wurube said, "Let the two of you stand together, and we will place our hands over your head and pray for the Spirit to come and be with you, and Father Gary can bless us all at the end of this prayer." And so Wurube, Dima, and Eiyo, like three prophets marching in from the desert, extended their arms over the heads of Julieta and Osura and prayed powerfully in Bari. When they had finished their prayer, Osura and Julieta likewise prayed, asking for healing and mutual forgiveness.

With my final blessing, it was like a three-day conference on love and peace had been concluded, and everyone started congratulating each other. And then I witnessed something I have rarely seen a Sudanese couple do in public: Osura took his wife into his big arms and hugged her, and Julieta, like a shy bride, put her arms around her husband.

I had a lot of time to think as Ratib and I drove along the long dusty road from Belameling to Adjumani. The day's events had only solidified my conviction that we find redemption in our lives by honoring our relationships. Married people know this; celibates know this; parents know this; communities of faith know this. What was stunning about this day for me was how remarkably and dizzyingly clear the intricacy of these relationships became in our unraveling of the problem at hand and our search for the truth. In that intimate and loving confrontation, I saw the love between two people, the love of the community for its brother and sister, and the love of God for all. We are each relational beings, because our Creator is relational. We need intimacy with another, intimacy with community, and intimacy with God. Without these intimacies, we are unmoored, left to float away from what is best in ourselves. And no matter how awful we have behaved or how blinded we have been by another's hurtful behavior or our own self-importance, we are redeemed in uncovering the beauty of our relationship. That day in Belameling, I was taught this truth once again, by Osura and Julieta and by the faithful attending of Wurube, Dima, and Eiyo.

Journal: June 2005

Triumph

Having completed a seminar on the sacraments in Munu, I joined Ratib in the pickup, and we set off for home. As we gunned through the elephant grass and soupy mud on the narrow village access road, a cheerful little group of laughing and hollering children ran behind us at a safe distance, accompanying us to the main road.

The long ride back to Adjumani was a quiet time for me. There was much on my mind. Sometimes I am struck by what has happened to me: how strange and mysterious it is that I should be here, sharing in the life of such wonderful people, living in a world that I could only have imagined not too many years ago. (Could I even have imagined it?) I am conscious of the fact that I—who at one time lived a life totally oblivious to God, to faith, and to church—am now bopping along the roads of northern Uganda because, one way or another, God has benevolently won my heart, and I choose to talk about that love with my life. I am like a ship whose sails were caught by a strong wind from an unfamiliar direction, a wind whose power was not known to me until that moment, and I slowly turned with dignity and pointed toward a new destination. It is such a mystery to me, even now, after all these years. What kind of love am I talking about? I don't know; I cannot express it but can only point to it. As Ratib and I moved through Moyo and pressed forward toward the Nile, words echoed in my head, knocking gently on my brain:

> He made me into a sharpened arrow,
> and concealed me in his quiver. (Isaiah 49:2)

I was concealed. And now, removed from the quiver, have I been shot into the Nile valley?

We reached the Nile (changing a flat tire along the way), took the ferry across, and, three hours after leaving Munu, hit the outskirts of Adjumani. A few minutes later, we pulled into the JRS compound. I thanked Ratib for another job flawlessly done and sent him on his way. Then I had a cold shower and a cold beer. What a deal.

The Face of Poverty

Jame, one of my catechists, from Lojili village, wanted to speak to me in private. He is a shy young man, between thirty and forty years old, a rookie among those catechists who have attended the training school. He is a humble man—I notice that every time he teaches he asks one of the other trained catechists present for feedback on his teaching, on both its substance and style. I always tell him not to get stuck in a book (it is always a temptation), but to teach what he knows and to do what he does best: ask good and provocative questions of his audience. His people are receptive to this, because they trust him.

Some of my top catechists and I had spent the day in the central Palorinya village of Masaloa. I walked outside with Jame, and there, sitting under a tree next to my pickup, was his wife, Mary. She was eight months pregnant; it would be their third child. The problem was that they needed medicine: could I help them? The clinics in this country are theoretically free, but often they are "out" of medicine, which means refugees are forced to buy it at a commercial outlet—an outlet that, incidentally, might be owned and run by employees of the clinics. Mary was even shier than Jame, because she spoke no English. She had walked about three miles to Masaloa from Lojili, figuring I needed to see her to believe there was a problem. I assured her that I would be happy to help and told them to seek me out after the birth should they need more assistance.

The requests for assistance pounce on me throughout the day, every day: Dima, another catechist, needs money to repair a bike; a woman leader asks for help to reconstruct her burned-down tukul; Matilde's son has finally finished driving school but is short on money for the driving permit; a student will be forced to drop out of secondary school unless she comes up with fifteen dollars; a family is without food; a child needs money for shoes; someone needs travel money to attend an uncle's funeral; a family needs money to provide food for a loved one at the hospital. So it goes, day after day, week after week. It wears me down, sometimes punching my impatience button, and a kind of anger aneurysm develops. I am angry especially when I feel people are making a request not so much out of need but because they figure I can get them what they want.

But this anger does not last, because it does not make sense. There was a time when I was a tightwad in these situations, even sanctimonious about "the proper use of funds." Now such an attitude is pitifully unconvincing, especially when I am staring into the ugly face of poverty. These people, my people, have no job opportunities, no resources, and find themselves up against a wall and screwed by life.

Ultimately I believe that it is not possible to be too generous in this world; it is not likely that I can go wrong in providing for someone if the money is available or the budget can be stretched to accommodate a person in need. In the refugee world, I am not dealing with professional scammers or thieves who have bank accounts full of money. I'm dealing with the likes of a young man, his pregnant wife, and their two hungry children, who have been driven from their country by civil war, have no government protection, and live on unproductive land with few options to earn a living.

Often here, I see with two sets of eyes. I see the endless disadvantages and deprivations of the refugees, the empty hands and stomachs in the villages; and simultaneously I see the abundance of the developed world, a world from which I come, where people are expected to accumulate, not relinquish, material goods. This double vision haunts me. But once I have held a Jame and a Mary in my arms, there is no way I can walk away from what I am seeing; there is no way I can not reject the injustice and the madness of the unequal distribution of the world's resources. It seems to me that Jesus had two sets of eyes as well: he saw the poor and the blind and the sick and the rejected, struggling in their lives of privation, even as he saw the condescending and condemning stares of the Pharisees who would maintain religious propriety and forget the human being. And he took his stand for the least. When I see side by side the haves and the have-nots, my vision becomes keener, and I'm more receptive to the cry for help, and to the heart of Christ in the ones who cry.

Juma and Calisto

I stopped at Okusijoni village to pick up Juma Santo; he and Calisto and I were doing a seminar in Agojo, and his compound was on the way. They would be teaching on the Eucharist, using a number of visual aids to help the people understand the subject matter. They are both trained and skilled in this method of teaching. Juma is probably the smartest of all the catechists in the Adjumani settlement and is comfortable with several languages. For diocesan meetings of catechists, primarily those from Ugandan parishes, he is often chosen to represent his brother and sister refugee catechists from the settlement. His chapel is well organized, and he is famous for always starting Sunday Prayers at 10:00 exactly—this in a world where starting on time is rare. This may be because people move by the sun here, not by the watch. Juma has a watch. He is in his late forties and was a teacher in Sudan before he fled. Like many refugees, he and his wife live off the land and monthly UNHCR provisions of maize and oil.

When I arrived, Juma was holding his sleepy-eyed baby, loaded on quinine, a treatment for malaria. Margaret, his wife, was bathing, so we waited in his compound: a few tukuls, a bathing place, a latrine, a building where he keeps supplies.

He and Margaret have lost three of their six children; in fact, a few years ago, two children died, a one-year-old to malaria and a four-year-old to meningitis, on the same day. Poverty: it is why Juma's baby is sick, why so many Sudanese and Ugandan children die prematurely. No matter the personal sacrifice I make, I can always fall back on the privileges of affluence: an educated background, a cold beer and tasty bread and a hot shower in Kampala, a transportation system and ready access to medical care in the States. Juma and his dear wife know nothing of these things. I love them in all their courage to stake out their lives creatively in the midst of the refugee world. One truth becomes more and more a part of me: being with the poor keeps me honest, even as I hate poverty's unholy existence.

I usually have Calisto work with Juma in the villages, because they are both Acholi, and their teaching styles complement each other. Calisto is about fifty and is married with four children. He has been a catechist since the age of twenty-five, when he was appointed to be one in Sudan, before he fled. I consider him to be the most pious of all the Adjumani catechists, but not in a stuffy or contrived way. He is simply a prayerful man. He is especially skilled in the instruction of young children. Out of the small amount he makes growing and selling crops, he manages to send his children to school.

Both of these good men are comfortable with me, as I am with them. I have trained them in the teaching of theology so that whether I am here or not, the local church is owned by its people, and people are being taught in their own language with their own symbols and images.

My love for Calisto and Juma grew as I watched them teach their hearts out on the Eucharist to an enthralled chapel. Imagine: one o'clock in the afternoon, the temperature over a hundred degrees, and a packed house of interested and appreciative villagers. Where is the purity of the Holy Spirit today? I know one place: an obscure chapel on an obscure day in obscure Agojo.

The Tears of Rose Adoo

I saw you struggling in your blood as I was passing, and I said to you as you lay in your blood: Live, and grow like the grass of the fields.

—Ezekiel 16:6–7

Rose and Lillian took the bus to Adjumani from their school in Arua, a dusty seven-hour trip. I have known them both for years, since I began my work with JRS at the Rhino Camp Refugee Settlement. They are Sudanese refugees, and I am like a father to them, especially Lillian, who is an orphan. I have assisted them with school fees and expenses over the years, raising money and using my own JRS salary with the permission of my superiors.

Rose and Lillian had come to visit me in Adjumani to talk about school and life. And, too, we wanted to see each other a final time: I would be leaving Africa soon.

After dinner with my community, Rose and I talked. She is twenty, a Madi by tribe, with a gleaming shaved head, large sensitive eyes, and a thoughtful smile. She communicates with an economy of words; having faced so many difficulties in her life, she is used to having to think things through quickly and make on-the-ground decisions. The eldest of five children—one of whom, a sister, is paraplegic and wheelchair bound—she and her family escaped from the war in Southern Sudan and were settled by the UNHCR in the village of Ocea, a poor, harsh village in the Rhino Camp settlement. The fabric of life for most refugee parents is torn by the loss of one or more children. In Rose's case, two of her brothers have died of malaria.

Rose eagerly and systematically filled me in on her schoolwork and then reflected on the future. She is interested in working in community development, which is a growing need in Southern Sudan now that peace has been achieved. As she was talking, her eyes suddenly filled with tears and she crouched forward, covering her face with her blue handkerchief. She wept.

I waited. These did not seem to be tears of grief. I knew that she had stumbled upon an inner truth, and its size and power and grace had simply seized her. Slowly lifting her head, she fixed me with a look that went straight to my heart.

She said, "I'm sorry, Father; I'm not crying because of sadness. It is just that I am so happy and grateful that I am sitting here with you talking about school and the future. My life could have been much different."

Indeed, things could have been very different for Rose. In fact, at one time, the notion of finishing school seemed like an impossible wall to climb. I met Rose early in that process of climbing. I was conducting a seminar for the catechists of several villages, and Rose had been hired as one of the cooks. Normally at these seminars, a few local women hired by the village chairman prepare lunch for the participants. She was fifteen at the time, ready to begin Quiver Secondary School, the only secondary school in the Rhino Camp settlement. It was a poor school with unqualified teachers that always ranked low on national standardized test results. She wanted to cook at the seminar because she would earn a little extra money for school.

She came to me during the seminar and asked if I could help her buy a calculator. She could use it in her science and math courses and loan it to the many students who could not afford one.

I bought her a calculator. It cost seven dollars.

For the next two years, she would periodically come to me and ask for assistance, although she didn't request much, because she grew maize and peanuts for sale. Her father also helped if he could land a construction job. She was the first girl in her clan to complete the seventh grade and therefore the first to go on to secondary school. The cultural attitude here is that education is for boys, but Rose's father, Isaac, a catechist and a skilled builder of tukuls, rejected this mentality and insisted that his girls would go to school, much to the astonishment (and joy) of his wife. His brothers, Rose's uncles, on the other hand, couldn't believe what their brother was doing; there were many men lined up to marry the bright and fetching daughter of Isaac. Surely he must know that she would bring a very high dowry? Isaac knew. So did Rose, and she loved her father for his stance. She wanted no part of the dead-end life of an arranged marriage at an early age that had been inflicted upon many of her friends.

I left Rhino Camp at the outset of Rose's fourth year at Quiver for the JRS pastoral assignment in Adjumani, north and across the Nile from Rhino Camp. One day, midway through my first year there, I returned from a visit to a settlement village to find Rose waiting for me at the gate of the JRS offices. She had biked fifty miles from Rhino Camp.

"I need to see you, Father."

In the office, I gave her a glass of water. Then she put her proposal to me plainly and boldly. Would I help her in the next phase of her schooling? She had finished O, or Ordinary, Level (the four-year secondary school program) and wanted to go on to A, or Advanced, Level (an additional two years of secondary school). But the school was in Arua, far from Rhino, and she had little money.

"Will you help me?" she asked. "It will be a boarding school and difficult, but I know I can pass the entrance requirements. I have done well at Quiver."

The school would cost about three hundred dollars a year, a fortune for her and her family.

So there we were again, although this time it was not a calculator that she needed, but money to attend a quality educational institution with a competent teaching staff. The studies would be difficult, and she would be faced with the challenges of being a Sudanese refugee in a predominantly Ugandan school, with only a handful of her tribe (Madi) attending.

"I know I can do it, Father, if I just have a chance," she repeated. "In the last year at Quiver, I was struggling for school fees, and the administration finally sent me away in the final term because I had not paid the balance of term fees of fifteen thousand shillings [about nine dollars]. And so my father hired himself out to dig in the fields in the hottest weather to make the necessary money." She sobbed softly, holding a handkerchief to her eyes. "He is an old man; it is difficult work. He has done this all his life for me and my sisters in order to take care of us. His sacrifice meant I could finish Quiver."

I didn't hesitate. "Okay," I told her. "Let's see if we can figure it out."

I recruited Atibuni, a staffer with the JRS project in Rhino Camp settlement and one of my dear friends, to help Rose with the application to the Muni School for Girls in Arua. He knew Rose and spoke Madi and English fluently. I rustled up the necessary funds from friends abroad and took money from my own salary. Rose was one of four Rhino Camp settlement girls, including Lillian, whom I assisted with schooling fees.

Weeks after her visit to Adjumani, Rose and Atibuni communicated to me that she had been accepted into the A level at Muni. Each term break she was to return to the Rhino Camp settlement and report to Atibuni. Then she would be off to her home in Ocea, where she would assist her family in the gathering of crops and her mother with household tasks and the care of her disabled sister.

Rose's second year at Muni began brightly, but before she could really get going she was diagnosed with tuberculosis, which she probably picked up in the village. About the same time, she was hit with typhoid fever, a bacterial disease that results in ripping headaches and persistent abdominal pain. Like most refugees, she resisted going to a doctor, fearing the expense. Finally, Lillian convinced her to see a doctor, knowing that I would help. The subsequent treatment and recovery interfered with school, and though she finished strong, she and Atibuni and I felt that she should repeat the year.

As we neared the end of our conversation, Rose looked at me happily, well into that repeat year, with the prospect of attending university down the line. She flashed a shy smile. And then, in her striking clipped English, she let loose with this salvo: "Father, I love you; my family loves you; Lillian and Mary and Edina love you. God has brought you and those who help you, and now we can say that we have not only survived but that we have a chance, an equal chance to grow as a woman in our culture—independent, strong, a source of joy and pride to our families."

Her lip quivered. She brought her handkerchief again to her face.

"I thank God," she whispered.

I pulled out *my* handkerchief, her tears calling to mine. I held her free hand in my free hand and didn't say anything. In the presence of such fierce heart talk, words seemed superfluous and dumb. I thought, *My God, what a good woman*, and I whispered a prayer of gratitude that Rose had been brought into my life.

Rose had survived her ordeal of fighting for an education and had come out on the other side as a woman in bloom. I thought of the tulips I saw in Ottawa emerging from the frozen ground after an impossibly cold winter. How many times have I walked in the quiet evenings of northern Uganda and looked back at my life's convolutions and wondered that I had come through it all. And wept, just as Rose had wept:

"Thank you, O God, thank you." It is not just that we survive through dark moments; it is that we come out okay. And it is not just that we come out okay, but that we are aware of God's presence in the whole tumbling process.

Early one cold winter morning, while driving along the Oregon coast, I hit black ice on a downgrade, spun around on the road, and went crashing into a ditch. I was left hanging upside down in my car, surrounded by broken glass, a caved-in roof, and what was left of the dashboard. But I was intact. I crawled out through the shattered glass of the passenger side door, shaken but alive.

I realized later in the day that the incident was a metaphor for my life: whether I was extracting myself from a wrecked car or coming out of the wreckage of bad choices or busted love or disillusionment, there had always been a solicitous Love present—a Love that desires me—furiously burning at the center of my being, calling me forward. Rose trusted that experience: God would be with her in all her troubles. God is present—"somehow," as the Sudanese are fond of saying. I know this; the presence of God in my life is an inner driving and loving force that is as real as breathing. The people in the refugee villages know this, even as they are surrounded by hunger and war; recovering alcoholics know this, looking back on their days of drinking madness; converts to Christianity know this, standing in the light that dispels the darkness. Rose knew this.

She and Lillian left Adjumani the next day. We knew that we would most likely not see each other again. As she boarded her bus, she handed me this letter:

> Dear Father Gary,
>   Departing, departing is so painful, Father, so what can I do but all in all wish you a safe journey back home.

May God bless you for the love you have shown to me since you came to Africa to accomplish your work.

I will never forget you in my life, simply because without you I don't know what type of a girl I might have been in the future. I thank God so much for that. For your coming into my life. May God bless you there and your family too.

Do remember me in your prayer, too, as I do remember you here, Father. So all in all may the love of Jesus Christ be with you there and take care of you for ever and ever. Amen.

Thanks,

From your faithful and loving daughter,

Adoo, Rose

NB. Father, I don't have anything to give to you as a reward, but God will reward you for the work you have done.

Journal: August 2006

Catholic Action

I have spent two days in the Palorinya village of Dongo, observing and supporting three catechists as they led a seminar for Catholic Action members from five different villages. The Catholic Action people attend to those in their village who are vulnerable: the sick, the physically and mentally disabled, and the elderly. The men and women who make up the Catholic Action group are crucial to the spiritual and physical health of the village. And when the village catechist is not available, they are also responsible for burying the dead.

There were thirty Bari women and men in attendance at the seminar. After three years, this would be my last such meeting in Palorinya. Domenica, a sharp and resourceful Ugandan catechist, facilitated the meeting, assisted by two refugee catechists. The discussion on how to help the vulnerable people of the villages was spirited and united.

First, Domenica presented helpful principles to the people—for example, the importance and dignity of all—which she rooted in Scripture; in this case, the passage from Matthew 25 about the least of the brothers and sisters. Then she asked, "What does this mean for you? Who was Jesus talking about? And who are the least of the brothers and sisters in your village?" The people talked about this and, in the process, gained a deeper understanding of the Scripture. Then Domenica asked them how they were to respond to the truth of this idea in their community. How were they to care for the least? Various ailments were discussed—blindness, mental illness, hunger, bacterial diseases, "slim disease" (AIDS)—and there were a lot of anecdotal details about the vulnerable in question. This was never gossipy, and Domenica stressed time and again that the vulnerable were part of the Body of Christ. The people always nodded in agreement on this point.

And the people also threw out questions of their own: How were they to confront and care for the alcoholics in their villages, some of whom were spouses of the Catholic Action members themselves? How were they to deal with mentally ill people who wandered around naked while their relatives didn't seem to care? And how were they to organize the youth to help get food to those who cannot grow their own crops? None of these questions or other frustrating situations were totally resolved, but the people had a chance to share in community, and the discussions gave them ideas on how to proceed in their own villages around a specific issue, project, or problem. Sudanese love to talk, and they could discuss one subject for an entire day.

My role in these meetings, beyond organizing the event and celebrating Mass at the conclusion of each day, was to back Domenica and the two assisting catechists and to be present in a way that was affirming of their efforts to understand their faith more deeply and share it with others.

After the final session and a meal, the women from the village of Morobi sang a song they had created for me, emphasizing the gift of love that I brought to the refugee people. The icing on the cake was the people's presentation to me of a twenty-pound bag of peanuts and a huge pumpkin—in typical fashion, they danced in two lines from the chapel to the eating area, carrying the gifts. Given the distant location of Dongo and the many miles most of the seminar participants had to travel, this was a very touching farewell present. One good woman came up to me and, with Ratib translating, said, "When my son grows up, I hope he is like you." I said, "Rather, like *you*."

As I near the end of my JRS work in Uganda, I feel the weight of responsibility and pressure dropping off me like stages of a rocket, the burden abated, the distance to the goal reduced, the forward motion more focused. The past six years have been like a marathon. There was the enormous amount of mental and physical preparation before the run, and then the huge amount of strength—of body and mind—measured out at various stages of the race. As the last mile comes up, I forget everything; I am just pushing myself toward and focusing on the finish line. I think less and rely on my instincts more. At the end, there will be the rush of knowing I made it, I did it, I conquered it. It's been a long run.

But although I am in the homestretch of my time in Africa, I will not stop running. There will be many more marathons, and each one will be informed and illuminated by this one. The highs and lows, the easy stretches and tough climbs, the moments of fatigue and those of exhilaration will stay with me. I will live always with the people and experiences and images of these past years in Africa, and they will cast their light on my future choices of service and love, as a Jesuit priest and as a human being.

Could I ever leave Africa permanently after all this? Should the final energies of my life be dedicated to the refugees of the world? For most people, these are not the questions. But they haunt me like a strain of music that I can't get out of my head.

The Final Gathering of the Adjumani Catechists

It was a picnic of giants, at least from my perspective. More than thirty catechists from twenty-five chapels made it to the picnic location in a jungle clearing overlooking the Nile. The good men and women present—

Kenyi, Tibi, Andruga, Madra, Hakim, Okaya, Aswan, Umbayo, Luka, Almaria, Avelino, Woja, Gama, Iga, Juma, Moga, Deng, Midyang, Modi, Latigo, Aju, Lagu, and Barua—had gathered to bid me farewell. Looking around at them as we talked and ate and danced and drank our beer, I heard a familiar song in my heart, the one that proclaims that the best of the church is discovered among the poor.

The acknowledged leader of the group, Juma, in the typically formal Sudanese manner, read a letter to me in front of everyone present. I include his words here not as a reflection on me, although they may be, but as an example of the quality of people that were given to me.

> Dear Reverend Fathers, Sisters, My Brother Catechists in Christ:
>
> I'm grateful to have this chance to extend my sincere appreciation to Rev. Father Gary Smith for the entire work he has done to Robidire parish.
>
> Father Gary has been full-time with us. He has been our Father in implementing our pastoral activity.
>
> Be like a father to orphans,
>   and as good as a husband to widows.
> And you will be like a son to the Most High,
>   whose love for you will surpass your mother's.
>   (Ecclesiasticus 4:10–11)
>
> Today let us pray for him so that the good Lord who brought him to us may also take him back safely. I know we are going to miss him in our facilitation team. We learned a lot from him.

May he send you help from the sanctuary,
give you support from Zion,
remember all your oblations
and find your holocaust acceptable;
may he grant you your heart's desire,
and crown all your plans with success;
may we shout with joy for your victory,
and plant our banners in the name of our God!
    (Psalm 20:2–5)

You have done well as Father. You have done that which the prophet Isaiah says:

The spirit of the Lord Yahweh has been given to me,
for Yahweh has anointed me.
He has sent me to bring good news to the poor,
to bind up hearts that are broken;
to proclaim liberty to captives,
freedom to those in prison;
to proclaim a year of favor from Yahweh,
a day of vengeance for our God.
    (61:1–2)

Our apostolate has been relying on you.

Let us continue to pray for him and for the one coming to succeed him so that we may continue with our program as usual. St. Paul says in his letter to the Ephesians:

Through him, both of us have in the one Spirit our way to come to the Father.

So you are no longer aliens or foreign visitors: you are citizens like all the saints, and part of God's household. You are part of a building that has the apostles and prophets for its foundations, and Christ Jesus himself for its main cornerstone. As every structure is aligned on him, all grow into one holy temple in the Lord; and you too, in him, are being built into a house where God lives, in the Spirit. (2:18–22)

So I want to say that in time of success or failure we must all be united.

Let us invoke the help of the saints and our mother Mary to guide Father Gary. Amen.

Thanks. Yours in Christ,

Juma Santo

I choked up a bit as I spoke to them in turn, sharing my gratitude for all they had given to me. I reminded them also that nothing will happen in the villages, indeed in the church, unless we are instruments of God willing to make things happen. That meant planning, preparing, studying, and loving our people, all the things we had been doing for the last three years.

I embraced each one before we left in the late afternoon. They were embraces attended by deep emotion.

Pasqualina

I celebrated one of my final Masses in Uganda today at Oliji, in the Adjumani settlement. It was a full house, with passionate singing by the choir and dancing by the Kizito during and after the Mass. Before I left the village, I went to see Pasqualina one last time. She is unable to move from the bed in her tukul as she approaches the final throes of AIDS. Her husband, who infected her, and two of her three children have already died from the disease. Sitting next to Pasqualina and under her mosquito net was her surviving daughter, a healthy girl, probably twelve years old. Across the tukul, Pasqualina's mother lay on a mat, sick from malaria.

Pasqualina in her dying was gracious, personable, simple, and direct. I sat on the floor next to her bed, and she reached her hand underneath the mosquito net to hold mine firmly. She looked at me with loving, tender eyes and told me that she would pray for me in this life and the next. And then she prayed, in clear English, for me and for my family in the States. She was present in a situation that would have broken most human beings and hurled them into a paroxysm of self-pity. Her thoughts at that moment were on God, her mother, her daughter, and me. I was a kindergartner listening to a PhD.

Oh, the obscurity of this moment, the holiness, the impossibility of it all. Did I come from the streets of Portland to be here, in this tukul, to learn from a dying woman the meaning of life—of my life? O God, watch over her tonight. Let her not suffer long.

Last Days in Palorinya

It was appropriate, I guess, that my final trip into the Palorinya Refugee Settlement would involve rain and its unmerciful partner, muddy roads. God knows how many days Ratib and I have battled muddy roads to Palorinya, depending on Ratib's skill to get us through. We were heading to Kali, where all the catechists were gathering for a final meeting with me.

As we came into the chapel area, located on a promontory overlooking the Nile, we were welcomed by the shouts of the wonderful gathering of catechists: Nyagong, Paride, Elia, Osura, Adie, Oluku, Abba,

Inja, Manja, Jansuk, Flabius, Severino, Binasio, Yugga, Donasio, Eiyo, Kenyi, Rokani, Munele, Sokiri, Modi, Marine, Wurube, Jame, Kiden, Dima, Lodu, and Chuan. I mention their names because each person is a memory and a story that occupies and owns a piece of my heart.

During the Mass, I told them that their journey was not complete, but during this interim in Uganda they had come to a better understanding of their faith and theology. It would prepare them for their return to Sudan and the development of the Sudan Church. At the conclusion of Mass, about twenty Kali women danced in from the back of the chapel, two of them bearing bags of maize and peanuts on their heads, gifts for me. I know that food is not in abundance in this area, so it was difficult and humbling to accept such offerings, but to refuse them would have been the worst kind of cultural impropriety. Sudanese have no problem combining sacrifice and love.

Finally, the head catechist, Wurube, thanked me for all that I had done and then prayed that God would send a priest to be with Wurube's flock. At that point, he asked me to stand in the middle of the chapel and invited all to surround me and impose their hands upon me in blessing. It was another unforgettable moment: being in the midst of people I love and recognized by their loving touch.

One of the women, Chuan, a young mother and a dear friend who possesses a mystical face, came to me, a sick child in tow. She was embarrassed to make a request at this time, but could I give her money to buy medicine for her three children, all struck by what sounded like the flu? Of course I could help. She needed seven thousand shillings—four bucks. Three children, four bucks. In all the joy of the occasion, this desperate plea broke my heart.

We came to the final good-bye. Everyone surrounded the pickup and then sent me on my way.

God's Sweet Gift

I did not sleep much last night because I was anxious about the liturgy at Magburu; it would be my final public Mass in Adjumani and the refugee settlements. I am used to anxiety in my work here, because I never know what is going to happen on a daily basis, but this was different. I remembered having a similar feeling at my first Mass in the Rhino Camp Refugee Settlement, six years ago, fretting about my pronunciation of the Bari language. I knew, of course, that today's nervousness was not over language deficiencies; it had to do with all the feelings I was having about my imminent departure. I asked to do this final Mass at Magburu because it is central to many of the villages and because of my special care for its people.

The Magburu chapel is in a spectacular location, opening out onto a panoramic view of the Nile valley. There are occasions when one can look out across the Nile and see gigantic storm clouds gathering like muscles. The chapel here is long, with mud-brick walls constructed by the people. One village carpenter built efficient swinging doors of coconut tree wood that can be secured when the chapel is not in use, preventing goats from wandering inside and stinking up the place. The grass for the chapel roof was purchased with the help of JRS.

When it was time for Mass, the Kizito dancers, twenty strong, led the procession, with catechists Samuel and Francesca flanking me. We ducked under the roof at the back of the chapel, entering a room full of kids dancing, people swaying, choir rocking, and women ululating. I was goose bumps. What is the language of goose bumps? What are they trying to say? I think they are alerting us to the presence of the sacred and the mysterious. My goose bumps were telling me that I was entering into a liturgy that is the sanctuary of the divine, and that liturgy would include at every moment an awareness of how far God has brought me and how wonderful the people are whom God has given me.

The Gospel was Mark 10:17–30, the dilemma of the rich young man who can't follow Christ because he is a man of great wealth. This reading was combined with Hebrews 4:12: "The word of God is something alive and active: it cuts like any double-edged sword but more finely." I spoke (Francesca, in her deep and comforting voice, translating) about God's power being alive and active, founding our faith and empowering us for the next step, which, in the case of the people of Magburu, implied the not-too-distant return to Sudan. To make that next step, we have to keep reminding ourselves of the priorities to which the Gospel calls our attention.

I had asked the teenagers of the chapel to do a drama depicting the rich young man of the Gospel. The people watched attentively as the person of wealth reluctantly abandoned what could give real wealth: following Christ. Interestingly, the young boy playing Christ became very sad as the young girl acting the role of the rich young man walked away. There was much applause when the drama was completed. This Gospel story is never a problem for the poor. This is not a group of people weighed down by the compulsions of wealth. Of course they would like to live in better conditions, have access to decent food and education for their children and a secure future. It is the abuse of money that they resist. No matter how much one possesses, the Gospel calls each of us to have a free heart.

After Mass I took questions from the floor about my family and why I am going. I know they are sad because they love me and do not want to see me leave. I feel this love and sadness everywhere lately, in all the villages and among the JRS staff. The refugees know that I came here because I wanted to come and that it entailed leaving my family. They understand that it is important and proper for me to return to my mother country and my family. Someone asked if I was leaving because I was sick. I told them I wasn't sick and then joked about how when an African adult suffers from malaria, he or she just keeps on working and moving, whereas the *mundu* (Madi for "white man") stays in bed and cries, cries, cries. Everyone nodded and laughed in agreement.

Then came a question that I did not know how to answer: "Will you come back to us?" I responded that I did not think I would, but ultimately, as they know, God is the one who sustains us, and if God chooses to bring me back to Africa through circumstances and superiors and the movements of my heart, then I would happily accept such a call. I also told them that I would always carry them in my heart, as a father and a mother carry within their hearts a distant child. All nodded at that truth; exiles know it much better than I do. The people applauded at the end of the question-and-answer session and gave the Swahili clapping gesture of gratitude, which concluded with all right arms pointed toward me, a snappy and happy blessing.

Before any post-Mass festivities, the catechists asked if I would anoint an aging sick woman in the village and bring her communion. I followed Samuel and Francesca and the woman's daughter to her compound, about a five-minute walk through a maze of tukuls. When we arrived, the daughter spoke to her mother and then invited the three of us inside. As I bent down and entered, I thought of how many times I had experienced this scene: an elderly person lying on a dirt floor, covered by a single blanket, the slight odor of urine in the air, and a fervent face bearing all the signs of final agony. And, too, the other familiar part of the scene: a loving child, her faithful daughter. I gave the woman communion and anointed her, and we all prayed together. On our way back to the chapel, the daughter, a grade-school teacher who spoke perfect English, told me of the family's escape fifteen years before from Sudan. Her father had died in the flight, and her mother had raised the children and sacrificed to get them through school.

Near the chapel, I made a stop at the tukul of my blind and crippled friend Yayo. As usual, she was bursting with joy as she welcomed me, ululating when she heard my voice calling her name and announcing in Arabic that I was there: "Ya-YO, Ya-YO, Ana fi, Ana fi." She clasped my hands as if she thought they would fall off if she let go. I gave her communion, and after a moment of prayer, she reached to take my hands again, wrapping them in her own thin and worn hands, gazing up at me with those wonderful blind eyes in inexpressible love. She knew that this would be our final time together. This is how I understand the biblical metaphor of being in the hands of God—here, with Yayo and the Yayos of the world, my hands in theirs. It is as if they are holding my heart. Hand in hand, heart in hand.

I proceeded to a tree that dominates the village and was led to a chair, where I was surrounded by hundreds of local people. At that point, the Kizito started singing and danced themselves from the chapel, in a line of two abreast, to my chair and then broke into four lines, all facing me. They sang welcoming songs for "Father Gary" in Madi and English and Lingala. Every so often, they would stop singing, and one would come forward and recite from memory a poem for the occasion.

The people of the chapel in Esia, a village about two miles north of Magburu, were also there. They began dancing in the exuberant Bari style, leaping vertically to the accompaniment of staccato clapping. Because the two villages intermingle all the time in the market, and the Madi of Magburu and the Bari of Esia marry, and their children attend the same primary school, the people of the two villages speak each other's language well enough to communicate. At the conclusion of the dancing, the catechist for the Esia chapel, Longa, gave a speech. He thanked the people of Magburu and then turned to me and said in Bari and then in English, "You are God's sweet gift to us, God's sweet gift of love."

Then a group of Magburu women danced through the crowd with gifts, singing in Madi, "We give you our blessing, Father Gary, and as you go back to your family, may you be a blessing for us." They carried a bag of eggs and a bound and bewildered rooster.

I remembered my ordination day decades before, when I lay prostrate in St. Ignatius Church at the University of San Francisco, listening to the Litany of the Saints, aware of the many friends there, including my family, who were not Catholic. I was aware, too, of my long journey from conversion to ordination. I asked God, rhetorically, *So are you really going to pull this off?* God continues to pull it off. There I was in the African bush, sitting next to the Nile, watching these Sudanese refugees dance their joy, give their gifts, and call my name.

Eventually, the festivities came to an end. As I walked toward the pickup, I pulled out my puppet, Scovia, and she and I waved good-bye to the children, who clapped gleefully, and thanked the huge crowd in Arabic and Madi. The people started singing a song, in English and Madi, the refrain of which was "Father Gary, don't worry, we are praying for you; Father Gary, don't worry, we are praying for you." Every time I remember this, I will weep. Surrounded by all the children, I thought that after all the good-byes in dozens of locations in Adjumani, Palorinya, and Rhino Camp, it came down to this final good-bye in Magburu.

So many memories came flying at me that it was difficult to stay focused. It is always a precious moment when one says good-bye to the beloved, because it is a moment that pivots out of hundreds of past experiences, informed by them and calling them to mind. My memories are like a sacred litany, like my own psalm that I can always pray to God: those first greetings of the Sudanese leaders at the Arua airfield; Lemi at dawn in Rhino Camp making me a father of his grown son, and Rebecca doing the same for her child, Chol; gifts of eggs, chickens, ducks, goats, cookies, peanuts, pumpkins, papayas, honey, mangos— even dishes of fried grasshoppers; my dear friend Atibuni; the fragile honesty shared between Osura and Julieta in my presence; Kony's dark cloud; baptisms at Tika; the dancing of the Dinka women; smiling children holding the hand of the *cawaja*; Yayo's joy; Jacelin's face; Moga's tears of love for his dead wife; the purity of faith on Christmas nights; the bishop's firm grasp of my hand when malaria incapacitated me; the tears of Rose Adoo; my own private concert presented by the singing children of Aliwara; the lepers of Arua; a baby girl named after my mother; the laughter of students; the singing of the women as we plowed through the bush in a pickup; the seminars in which people shared and came to a deeper understanding of their faith; my loyal and steady companion Ratib; every village and every catechist. And it goes on, a cherished forest of memories that stretches to the horizons of my inner landscape.

Sometimes it's hard to believe that all this happened to me. But it did.

Those Damn Jesuits

I am because we are; we are because I am.

—East African proverb

"Now, the Jesuits," my late mother asked me, "are they the same as the Catholic Church?"

"Well, yes, Mom," I responded. "They are not *the* Catholic Church, but *part* of the Catholic Church." I maintained a straight face, knowing, of course, that since the early stages of the Society of Jesus, there have always been critics calling us a rogue element in the Catholic Church, phony intellectual hotshots who operate on the fringes of Christianity. My mom, till the day she died, never figured out how to say "Jesuit"— she always said "Je-sue-it." Not being a Catholic or really interested in organized religion, she had never heard the word until I transferred from San Jose State to the Jesuit Santa Clara University. Ultimately, it didn't matter if she'd never heard of us—if I was happy, she was happy.

Common Mission Affirmed

Belonging to the Jesuits is a fact that a lot of us Jesuits take for granted. We aren't indifferent; it's just that we do our thing and don't make a big deal of it. Being a Jesuit is an ordinary fact of life. But there are occasions when being a Jesuit is not ordinary. A certain confluence of events casts light on our vocation and reminds us of the gifts and talents of the organization to which we belong. We appreciate those gifts and hold them close, knowing that our hearts have been uncovered in the presence of a group of outstanding individuals. Our brother Jesuits are frequently instruments of God who help us see the truth of our mission and the importance of our companionship.

I experienced such a juncture when my provincial, my superior in the Oregon province, came to see me near the end of my time in northern Uganda.

John spent thirty-six hours getting to me; his stop in Uganda was the last leg of a trip that had taken him from Oregon to Jerusalem to Zambia. It was a long trip and long planned, expensive and demanding. But when he landed at the Moyo airstrip, he jumped off the plane and took me into his arms, overjoyed to see me. It was Stanley finding Livingstone. Beyond my affection for him and my appreciation of his belief in me, I was stirred by his coming. For my superior to track me down in this faraway place was a wonderful affirmation of mission—my mission, the mission of the Jesuit Refugee Service, and the mission of the Jesuits worldwide to serve Christ and Christ's poor. I could never do what I do alone; even when I was alone in the African bush, I depended on my brother Jesuits and our lay companions around the world.

From the airstrip, we drove for an hour through Moyo to the chapel of Lojili. There we were greeted by singing women waving banners, scores of children, and all the catechists of the settlement and their spouses—all come to meet and honor the superior of Abuna Gary. John was for them a special kind of elder.

Inside the jam-packed chapel, I introduced John and told the people why he had come. Then I invited them to speak to him about the church in the refugee settlement and why they were catechists and believers—and, too, to ask questions of him. As is the Sudanese custom when a visitor is present, especially an elder, each of the fourteen catechists present welcomed John. I was immediately struck by two things as I listened to the people talk: first, their statements of faith in the midst of exile, and second, their comparing of the refugees to Abraham, coming into the unknown but believing that God was with them. They described how the faith was lived in each chapel, emphasizing hope and mutual care, and some spoke about the struggles of hunger, of drought, of not being a citizen, and of their children being deprived of a strong church life, which the civil war had weakened and impoverished. And they asked questions. Would John be sending more priests since Abuna Gary was leaving? How did the American Church view the church as it existed in Uganda and Sudan? Were Americans aware of the refugees? Did they know about the wars and the drought? Could money be sent to help the children through school?

John never dodged a question but answered them as best as he could; more important, he spoke with heart. The people picked up on this right away and knew that he wanted to be there with them. Then he spoke of the Body of Christ, saying that we are all part of it, and that was the truth that compelled him to come, to send me, and to look for ways in which the American Jesuits could help—not just the Sudanese refugees, but refugees throughout the world.

The meeting in the Lojili chapel was a spiritual moment for all present. I could tell that John saw a purity of faith that he had not seen before as the people of this simple chapel in the middle of the Ugandan bush told him the story of their faith. And the people were hearing the same story of faith expressed by two Jesuit priests from a totally different culture. It was a wonderful consolation for me, and one of those moments when I understood what happened at Pentecost. I was proud of my provincial and friend and proud to be a Jesuit.

The chapel exchange lasted for two hours and concluded with everyone in the chapel being served tea and sweet potatoes. Outside, the people began singing and dancing again—it was a visual for me of the word *happiness*. I think the occasion meant more to them than if the bishop or even the pope had come, because they knew me, worked with me, trusted me, taught me, laughed and wept with me, and John was the one who had sent me to them, sustained me with them, and now affirmed me with them, thereby affirming that the world had not forgotten them.

John and I returned to Adjumani and the next day had tea at a little place by the Nile. As I shared with him my convictions about working in Uganda and being with the poor, he was able to affirm me again, reminding me that this solidarity with the poor was the way Christ lived and was what the Jesuits put front and center in their apostolic documents. Our lives are incarnational; we imitate Christ when our love for the poor becomes flesh dwelling in the world.

The question of how to live in solidarity with the poor can be tough for us Jesuits. But again and again our documents and our leaders call us to take a deeper look at the meaning of poverty and solidarity with those who live it. And when we scratch the deepest place of our collective Jesuit heart, isn't this where we want to go—to the poor? Doesn't our blood contain the call of Christ to be with the least? The poor are the engines that drive us—we find ourselves in serving them and confronting their oppression. As Joseph Conwell, SJ, said in his book *Impelling Spirit*, "The Spirit leads wherever the children of God are in deeper need."

The world moves along shrewdly, pimping its idols of consumerism and greed and systematically creating a pervasive injustice in which the poor are disregarded. But the last place a Jesuit wants to be in the face of such cultural trivialization of the least of the brothers and sisters is on the sidelines, untouched, unmoved, deaf, blind. Our mission is to challenge that trivialization and create alternatives; our hearts call us to be torches carried or thrown into the world's darkness, whether we are on the streets or in the universities, in the parishes or in the high schools, with refugees or with coworkers.

Companions

Shortly after John's visit, I concluded my time with JRS and began my trip home. Frido, my companion in Adjumani, drove me to Entebbe Airport, outside Kampala. We had arrived together in the North three years before, he as the project director, and I as the pastoral coordinator. We lived and ate together, we talked and prayed together, we laughed and wept together. When he was down with malaria, I found him a doctor, and when I was down with malaria, he fussed over me until I was healthy. As we embraced at the airport, we both started to weep, Frido telling me, "You have been a wonderful companion, a wonderful brother."

In John's affirmation of me and Frido's care for me, I am struck once again by the importance in my life of my Jesuit brothers. Because of my Jesuit friends and brothers, I do not follow Christ alone. Because of them, I grow and share in a common vision of love and hope for the world. Because of them, I have people in my life who understand my search for truth. Because of them, I have a brotherhood that invites my creativity and nurtures my desire to try new things. Because of them, I know that my back is covered when I am betrayed, when I am in danger, when I am laughed at, and when I am judged as out of step with the human values of the world. I say this as a human being—a Jesuit priest—who recognizes the gifts of my brothers that enhance and ratify my mission and help me make sense of life.

As human beings, we Jesuits are fools and brains, painfully shy and irrepressibly extroverted, wisecracking and sensitive, spellbinding and boring, activists and bystanders, queen bees and workers, eagles and sparrows, stallions and donkeys. But I think that whatever our differences, we all try—sometimes successfully, sometimes not—to love, challenge, and support one another.

There is a little paperback, called *The Secret Terrorists*, that makes the rounds among the sidewalk vendors of Kampala. It is distributed by a virulently anti-Jesuit U.S.-based group and accuses the Jesuits of being the real terrorists of the world. A spectacular compilation of disconnected information, it "proves" that the Society of Jesus is responsible for terrorist attacks and has been working to destroy America, its Constitution, and everything for which America stands. I thought recently that if the authors of the book had seen John and I talking at the Moyo airstrip, his arm around my shoulder, or Frido and I embracing at Entebbe Airport, having our departing heart-to-heart, they would have had a field day, arriving swiftly at their foregone conclusion: *The Jesuits are plotting again. Those damn Jesuits are plotting again.*

Yep, I confess we are plotting. But there is nothing secret in our plot. It is this: to overthrow the world's duplicity with the truth of the gospel; to confront injustice with Christ's passion for the poor; to replace violence with peace; to go anywhere, anytime, and by any means to places where we can confront the heart of darkness with the heart of God.

Afterword

If you do away with the yoke,
the clinched fist, the wicked word,
if you give your bread to the hungry,
and relief to the oppressed,
your light will rise in the darkness
and your shadows become like noon.
Yahweh will always guide you,
giving you relief in desert places. . . .
You will rebuild the ancient ruins,
build up on the old foundations.
You will be called "Breach-mender,"
"Restorer of ruined houses."

—Isaiah 58:9–12

I grew up in the Central Valley of California on a narrow swath of land, a hundred miles long and fifty miles wide. It was my world. A carnival came to town one day, and I took my first ride on a Ferris wheel. At the topmost point, I had the bewildering experience of seeing beyond my hometown and beyond the surrounding fruit orchards. In one sweeping look, I took in the flat plain running north to south and the mountains that stood on either side of the valley. I had no idea that things were that big. Later in life, I wrote about that carnival ride:

Last night on the Ferris wheel I looked down upon the
   plain.
The world was so much different then; it will never be the
   same.

That vision became an enduring metaphor for change in me.
Experiences that gave me a new understanding of my past and future
life became Ferris wheel moments: the night I read the Gospel of
Mark and discovered the person of Jesus; the first time I ever heard
Miles Davis; the first time I stood on the shore of the Pacific Ocean;
my days as chaplain at a Toronto women's prison; my ordination to
the priesthood in San Francisco; my years on the streets with the
poor and homeless and mentally ill; every time I held a child dying of
malaria in my arms; the first time I walked into a refugee chapel and
was surrounded by a joyful deluge of singing and ululating. The list
goes on. We all have them.

These past several years have been the tallest Ferris wheels I have
ever been on. I look differently now on the plain of my life. What I see is
imbued with my experience of the Sudanese and the Ugandans and their
world, and I see my own culture, my own world, anew. How I think, how
I preach, and how I pray are all colored by Africa: I walk into a super-
market, and American abundance is contrasted with the deprivations of
the refugee villages; I see a child smile or walk into a hospital, and immediately the scene is replayed in my mind in an African context.

Furthermore, in these months since I have returned from Africa
to rest and write and recharge, it is clear to me that I am thinking differently about the future of the Society of Jesus and the church, and of
how the twenty-first century will be a time of profound change for both.
Africa, with its blazing energy and its different history and its multi-
plicity of cultures, will emerge and touch the entire Body of Christ. I
realize that I am eager to be in on that unfolding dynamic.

I'm anxious as I write. Notwithstanding all my optimism and convictions, there lurks a fear that I will lose my edge, that I will be numbed by the American culture and its material seductions. I wonder if I will become comfortable again and be nothing more than a stammering witness of what I have seen. Will I play it safe? Will I forget? Will I forget a world where poverty consumes entire countries; where whole cultures are without basic health care; where hunger is common and not an exception; where education is out of reach for millions of young people, especially women; and where there is so damn much suffering born of indifference and greed?

This thinking drives me to my knees and to a constant prayer for myself and the Society of Jesus and the church that the Holy Spirit will never let us forget. I pray that the Spirit will place in our hands the sharp sword of belief in and passion for Christ's truth, and constantly stoke God's fire in our bones, and give us a thundering indignation over the abuse of the forgotten people of the world.

Only God can work such a miracle.

I pray that we will be like Abraham and head into the unknown, into the big country of God, defying odds and propriety; that we will turn our face toward Macedonia like Paul, possessing a single-minded mission to preach the story of God's love manifested in Jesus until we drop dead; that we will be struck like Isaiah with the magnificent obsession to bring the Good News to the poor, to bind up broken hearts, and to release those bound unjustly, and—in living out that obsession—that we will rejoice that God calls us breach menders.

I move forward; I follow my heart. As a Jesuit, I make it known to my superior what I think my heart is being called to, in the context of the society's mission. That said, my heart will always lie with the refugees—they have confirmed for me that with them one can discover the best in him- or herself; they are the impelling force that God uses in my life to drive me to new changes and new growth. The future will be a response to this truth and to the inspirations of God and to the discernment of myself and my call as a Jesuit.

Now, like my Sudanese brothers and sisters leaning over a cup of water in thankful prayer, I hover over the cup of my life, giving thanks for what has been and asking for guidance. As I have changed and grown since those whisperings long ago in San Jose leading me to follow Christ, I trust that God will sustain me in the path ahead and continue to take me to the breaches.